TABLE OF CONTENTS

1. Introduction to SaaS Marketing 5
2. Understanding the SaaS Market 11
3. Defining Your SaaS Marketing Strategy 19
4. Building Your SaaS Brand 29
5. Creating a Content Marketing Plan 43
6. Implementing Inbound Marketing 55
7. Boosting MQL to SQL Conversion Rate in SaaS Marketing 67
8. Paid Advertising and Acquisition Channels 75
9. Customer Success and Retention 87
10. Measuring SaaS Success 105
11. Scaling and Growth Strategies 123
12. Future Trends in SaaS Marketing 135
13. Case Studies and Examples 145

14. Bonus Chapters

SaaS Marketing Mistakes and Solutions *151*

How to Raise Money for Your SaaS Idea *169*

Networking for Fund Raising *175*

General Valuation Methods *179*

Assessing the Growth Stage of Your SaaS Startup *189*

Cautions *193*

Chapter 1

INTRODUCTION TO SAAS MARKETING

Welcome to the world of SaaS marketing! In this chapter, we will explore what SaaS is and the unique challenges that SaaS companies face when it comes to marketing. We will also discuss why effective marketing strategies are crucial for the success of SaaS businesses. Let's dive in!

1.1 What is SaaS and its Unique Marketing Challenges?

SaaS stands for Software as a Service. It's a type of software delivery where you access and use applications through the internet instead of installing them on your computer. SaaS offers flexibility and scalability, but it also presents some specific challenges for marketing.

One challenge is that SaaS companies rely on recurring revenue. Instead of selling software once, they must keep customers subscribed to their services. This means they have to constantly engage and provide value to their customers to keep them coming back.

Another challenge is the competitive nature of the SaaS market. There are many companies offering similar services, so it's important for SaaS businesses to stay innovative and stand out from the crowd to attract and retain customers.

Challenge 1: Acquiring New Customers Solution: SaaS companies need to develop targeted marketing campaigns to reach their ideal customers. By identifying their target audience's pain points and showcasing how their software solves those problems, SaaS businesses can attract new customers. They can leverage various marketing channels, such as social media, content marketing, and paid advertising, to increase visibility and generate leads.

For example, Slack, a popular team collaboration software, effectively uses content marketing to target specific buyer personas. They create blog posts, webinars, and videos that address common workplace communication challenges, positioning their software as the solution.

Challenge 2: Customer Retention and Renewals Solution: SaaS companies must focus on customer success and ensuring a positive user experience. This involves providing excellent customer support, continuous product improvements, and ongoing training resources. By investing in customer success programs and demonstrating the value of their software, SaaS businesses can increase customer satisfaction and retention rates.

Salesforce, a leading SaaS CRM platform, offers extensive training materials, certification programs, and a robust support community to help its customers succeed. By empowering users with the necessary skills and support, Salesforce enhances customer satisfaction and encourages long-term relationships.

Challenge 3: Staying Innovative and Competitive Solution: SaaS companies need to stay ahead of the curve by continuously innovating and adapting to market trends. Effective marketing includes monitoring industry developments, analyzing competitors, and regularly updating their software to meet evolving customer needs. By showcasing their commitment to innovation and providing regular product updates, SaaS businesses can maintain a competitive edge.

A prime example is **Adobe Creative Cloud,** which offers a suite of software for design, photography, and video editing. They constantly release new features and updates, keeping their software fresh and appealing to their creative professional target audience.

However, the biggest challenge I face is when people mix up SaaS marketing with performance marketing. I would like to explain that SAAS marketing and performance marketing are two distinct approaches that businesses employ to achieve different objectives;

SAAS Marketing: SAAS marketing focuses on promoting and selling software-as-a-service (SAAS) products. It aims to create awareness, generate leads, and convert prospects into paying customers. SAAS marketing strategies typically revolve around showcasing the unique features and benefits of the software, addressing pain points, and positioning the product as a solution to specific customer needs. It involves a combination of inbound marketing techniques, content creation, lead nurturing, and customer retention strategies to build a loyal customer base. SAAS marketing is more long-term and relationship-oriented, aiming to establish a strong brand presence and maximize customer lifetime value.

Performance Marketing: Performance marketing, on the other hand, is a data-driven approach focused on maximizing immediate results and return on investment (ROI). It revolves around driving measurable actions or conversions, such as clicks, sign-ups, downloads, purchases, or other desired user actions. Performance marketing strategies often employ paid advertising channels, such as search engine marketing (SEM), display advertising, affiliate marketing, or social media advertising, to reach specific target audiences and achieve direct, measurable outcomes. The success of performance marketing campaigns is evaluated based on key performance indicators (KPIs) like click-through rates, conversion rates, cost per acquisition (CPA), or return on ad spend (ROAS).

In summary, SAAS marketing aims to build brand awareness, engage prospects, and nurture long-term customer relationships, while performance marketing focuses on immediate results and measurable actions. While SAAS marketing is more holistic and customer-centric, performance marketing is more focused on optimizing campaigns to achieve specific performance metrics. Both approaches have their merits and are often used in combination to drive overall business growth and success.

1.2 Why Effective Marketing Strategies Matter for SaaS Companies

Now, let's understand why marketing strategies are so important for SaaS companies. Effective marketing helps SaaS businesses differentiate themselves and get noticed by potential customers. It's like telling a compelling story that grabs people's attention and makes them want to learn more.

For example, think about a popular SaaS company like **Dropbox.** They used effective marketing strategies to showcase the benefits of their cloud storage service. By offering free storage and incentivizing users to refer their friends, they were able to attract millions of customers and grow rapidly.

Marketing strategies also play a crucial role in acquiring and keeping customers. By creating targeted campaigns, SaaS companies can reach the right audience and convince them to sign up for their services. They can also use marketing techniques to nurture customer relationships, provide support, and ensure customer satisfaction.

A great example of this is **HubSpot,** a leading SaaS company providing marketing and sales software. They offer valuable content, such as blog posts and free educational resources, to attract and engage their target audience. Through their inbound marketing approach, they build trust and establish themselves as industry experts, which ultimately leads to more customers and business growth.

However, there are numerous examples of the companies listed below (some of which are frequently covered in the news) that have experienced failure primarily due to poor marketing. Interestingly, many of these companies are observed to have a SAAS brand manager from a prestigious business school or with prior experience in the marketing industry. Some of these are mentioned below;

1.2.1 Stayzilla (India, Failed in 2017):

Stayzilla was an online marketplace for homestays and budget accommodations in India. The company faced challenges in scaling its operations and attracting sufficient demand. Despite marketing efforts, Stayzilla struggled to compete with established players and ultimately shut down.

1.2.2 Jolla (Finland, Failed in 2017):

Jolla was a mobile operating system developer that aimed to offer an alternative to iOS and Android. One of their marketing mistakes was targeting a niche market without achieving sufficient developer support and app availability. This limited ecosystem support hindered their ability to attract users and compete with established mobile platforms, resulting in their failure.

1.2.3 Restopolitan (France, Failed in 2019):

Restopolitan offered a subscription-based dining service that provided discounts at partner restaurants. Despite marketing campaigns and a unique value proposition, the company struggled to retain subscribers and generate sustainable revenue. Restopolitan ultimately closed down its operations.

1.2.4 Homejoy (USA, Failed in 2015):

Homejoy offered on-demand home cleaning services through a mobile app. Despite a strong value proposition, their mistake was relying heavily on discounted promotions and coupon-based marketing to attract customers. This resulted in unsustainable pricing and profit margins, making it challenging for Homejoy to sustain its operations and compete with other home cleaning service providers

1.2.5 Clinkle (USA, Failed in 2016):

Clinkle aimed to revolutionize mobile payments by offering a unique payment app. However, their marketing mistake was creating excessive hype and secrecy around thcir product, without delivering a compelling and differentiated solution. This led to high expectations that were not met, resulting in a loss of user interest and ultimately the failure of the company

1.2.6 Ouya (USA, Failed in 2015):

Ouya was a video game console that aimed to disrupt the gaming industry by offering an open-source platform for indie game developers. However, their mistake was insufficient marketing efforts to attract both developers and gamers to the platform. The lack of compelling games and limited developer support resulted in low user adoption, leading to the downfall of Ouya.

These examples illustrate the importance of effective marketing strategies in the success of SAAS companies. Mistakes such as poor content promotion, lack of ecosystem support, relying on unsustainable pricing, not addressing user concerns, inadequate differentiation, excessive hype, and neglecting partnerships can all contribute to the failure of SAAS companies in the competitive market.

In summary, effective marketing strategies help SaaS companies stand out, attract customers, and build lasting relationships. By telling a compelling story and using targeted campaigns, SaaS businesses can overcome the challenges they face and achieve success in the competitive SaaS market.

This chapter sets the stage for the rest of the book, where we will go deeper into specific SaaS marketing strategies and techniques. Get ready to discover how to navigate the world of SaaS marketing and unlock your business's potential for success in the digital age!

CHAPTER 2

UNDERSTANDING THE SAAS MARKET

In this chapter, we will deep dive into the world of the SaaS market and gain a comprehensive understanding of its landscape. We will explore the key elements that make up the SaaS market, including target customers, niches, competition, and market trends. By the end of this chapter, you will have a solid foundation for developing effective marketing strategies in the SaaS industry. Let's dive in!

2.1 Overview of the SaaS Market Landscape

To navigate the SaaS market successfully, it's crucial to have a clear understanding of its landscape. The SaaS market is characterized by a wide range of software applications delivered as services over the internet. This model offers businesses and individuals the convenience of accessing software without the need for complex installations or maintenance.

The SaaS market encompasses various industries, including customer relationship management (CRM), project management, human resources, marketing automation, and more. Each industry has its own unique dynamics, target audience, and competitive landscape. Understanding the overall landscape helps SaaS companies identify opportunities and position themselves strategically within their chosen niche.

For instance, let's consider the CRM industry. Companies like Salesforce, HubSpot, and Zoho compete in this space by offering cloud-based CRM solutions that streamline sales and customer management processes. By understanding the overall CRM market landscape, these companies can differentiate themselves based on their features, pricing, target market, or specialized functionalities.

Another example can be of the cloud industry is a rapidly growing sector within the SaaS market. Companies such as Amazon Web Services (AWS), Microsoft Azure, and Google Cloud Platform dominate this space by providing infrastructure-as-a-service (IaaS), platform-as-a-service (PaaS), and software-as-a-service (SaaS) solutions. These cloud providers offer scalable computing resources, storage, and a wide range of cloud-based services to businesses of all sizes. Understanding the competitive landscape of the cloud industry enables companies to differentiate themselves based on factors like security, reliability, pricing models, and specialized offerings, allowing them to cater to specific customer needs and gain a competitive edge.

2.2 Identifying Target Customers and Niches

To effectively market a SaaS product, it's essential to identify and understand the target customers and niches. Target customers are the specific groups of individuals or businesses that are most likely to benefit from and purchase your SaaS offering.

One way to identify target customers is through the development of buyer personas. Buyer personas are fictional representations of your ideal customers, based on research and data. By creating detailed profiles of your target customers, including their demographics, needs, pain points, and goals, you can tailor your marketing messages and strategies to resonate with them effectively.

For example, if your SaaS product is an email marketing automation tool, your target customers could be small-to-medium-sized businesses that heavily rely on email marketing to engage their audience. By understanding their challenges, such as limited resources or lack of technical expertise, you can position your SaaS product as a solution that simplifies and optimizes their email marketing efforts.

Example

Company: HubSpot

SaaS Product: Inbound Marketing and Sales Software

Target Customers and Niches:

1. **Small and Medium-sized Businesses (SMBs):** HubSpot offers a user-friendly, all-in-one marketing solution for SMBs with limited resources and marketing expertise. They address lead generation, CRM, and social media marketing pain points.

2. **Marketing Agencies:** HubSpot provides an agency-focused platform for marketing agencies, streamlining client management, campaign tracking, and reporting processes.

3. **E-commerce Businesses:** HubSpot caters to e-commerce businesses with features like integrated shopping carts, personalized recommendations, and abandoned cart recovery.

By understanding the specific needs of these target customers and niches, HubSpot tailors their marketing strategies and product features to effectively position their SaaS product in the market.

Furthermore, within the SaaS market, there are often specific niches or specialized segments that present unique opportunities. By identifying and targeting these niches, SaaS companies can focus their marketing efforts on specific industries, geographic locations, or customer segments that have distinct needs or preferences.

2.3 Analyzing Competition and Market Trends

Understanding the competitive landscape and market trends is essential for effective SaaS marketing. Analyzing your competitors helps you identify their strengths, weaknesses, market positioning, pricing strategies, and unique selling points. This information allows you to differentiate your SaaS offering and develop a compelling value proposition that resonates with your target customers.

Conducting a competitive analysis involves researching and gathering information about your direct and indirect competitors. Direct competitors offer similar SaaS products within your industry, while indirect competitors provide alternative solutions that may address similar customer needs.

In addition to analyzing competition, staying up to date with market trends is crucial for adapting your marketing strategies and staying ahead of the curve. Market trends can include shifts in customer preferences, emerging technologies, regulatory changes, or evolving industry practices. By monitoring and leveraging these trends, you can identify new opportunities, anticipate customer needs, and position your SaaS product for long-term success.

For instance, the rise of artificial intelligence and machine learning has influenced the SaaS market in various ways. SaaS companies have started integrating AI capabilities into their products to enhance automation, personalization, and data analysis. By embracing these trends, SaaS companies can offer innovative solutions that meet the changing needs of their target customers.

Usually, if you do PESTLE or SWOT to understand the business model of a competitor, then most of thing which most the SaaS product manager skip is to understand industry visa vis the business and revenue generation model of their closest competitor.

Now let's look at some of these frameworks;

One of the frameworks that has worked for me while managing software saas sales is PROFIT Framework (as it's an acronym, all the sales team members can easily remember and follow it delivering great business results quater on quater)

Another popular framework is SWOT. It's an age-old framework but still very effective. SWOT analysis is a structured approach that involves evaluating the internal strengths and weaknesses of a business or organization, along with the external opportunities and threats it faces. Here are the steps to conduct a SWOT analysis:

1. **Identify strengths:** Begin by examining the internal factors that give your business a competitive advantage. These can include unique features, strong brand recognition, skilled employees, valuable intellectual property, or efficient processes. Make a list of all the strengths that set your business apart from competitors.

2. **Assess weaknesses**: Evaluate the internal factors that may hinder your business's performance or put it at a disadvantage. Consider areas where your business may have limitations, such as outdated technology, lack of resources, inadequate skills, or inefficient processes. Identify areas where improvements can be made and list them as weaknesses.

3. **Explore opportunities:** Look externally at the market and industry trends to identify potential opportunities for your business. Consider factors such as emerging technologies, changing customer preferences, new market segments, or gaps in the competition. Determine how your business can leverage these opportunities to grow, expand its market share, or introduce new products or services.

4. **Analyze threats:** Examine the external factors that could pose challenges or threats to your business. This may include factors like increasing competition, economic downturns, changing regulations, or shifts in consumer behavior. Identify potential risks that could impact your business negatively and consider strategies to mitigate them.

5. **Evaluate and prioritize**: Once you have compiled the lists of strengths, weaknesses, opportunities, and threats, evaluate each item and prioritize them based on their relevance and potential impact on your business. Focus on the items that are most significant and require immediate attention or strategic action.

6. **Develop strategies**: Based on the insights gained from the SWOT analysis, develop strategies that capitalize on strengths, minimize weaknesses, exploit opportunities, and mitigate threats. These strategies should align with your business objectives and help you achieve your goals.

Remember that a SWOT analysis is not a one-time exercise. It should be periodically reviewed and updated to reflect changes in the internal and external business environment. By regularly conducting a SWOT analysis, you can stay proactive, adapt to market dynamics, and make informed decisions to drive the success of your business.

In summary, understanding the SaaS market landscape involves gaining insights into target customers, niches, competition, and market trends. By identifying target customers and niches, analyzing competition, and staying aware of market trends, SaaS companies can develop effective marketing strategies that resonate with their audience, differentiate their offerings, and capitalize on emerging opportunities

In the next chapter, we will explore into the process of defining your SaaS marketing strategy, setting goals, and developing buyer personas. Get ready to take your SaaS marketing efforts to the next level!

Notes

CHAPTER 3

DEFINING YOUR SAAS MARKETING STRATEGY

In order to effectively market your SaaS product, it's crucial to define a comprehensive marketing strategy. This chapter will guide you through the key components of developing a solid SaaS marketing strategy, including setting marketing goals and objectives, developing buyer personas for effective targeting, and creating a unique value proposition.

3.1 Setting Marketing Goals and Objectives:

Setting clear and measurable marketing goals and objectives is essential to drive your SaaS marketing strategy in the right direction. These goals serve as benchmarks for evaluating the success of your marketing efforts. Here are some examples of marketing goals and objectives for a SaaS company:

a) **Increase Brand Awareness:**

- **Objective:** Increase brand recognition and reach by expanding social media presence and online advertising campaigns.
- **Goal:** Achieve a 20% increase in website traffic and a 10% growth in social media followers within six months.

b) Generate Qualified Leads:

- **Objective:** Implement lead generation strategies, such as content marketing and SEO optimization, to attract and capture potential customers.
- **Goal:** Achieve a 30% increase in qualified leads per month through website forms and gated content downloads.

c) Improve Customer Retention:

- **Objective:** Enhance customer satisfaction and reduce churn rate by implementing customer success programs and personalized communication.
- **Goal:** Achieve a 15% decrease in churn rate and increase customer retention by 20% over the next year.

By setting specific, measurable, attainable, relevant, and time-bound (SMART) goals, you can align your marketing efforts and track your progress effectively.

3.2 Developing Buyer Personas for Effective Targeting:

Buyer personas are fictional representations of your ideal customers. They help you understand your target audience's demographics, behaviors, pain points, and goals, enabling you to tailor your marketing messages and strategies to resonate with them effectively.

1. **Creating detailed customer personas** allows businesses to improve their marketing strategies by customizing their messaging, products, and services to meet the specific needs of their target audience. The following steps provide a comprehensive framework for developing accurate and impactful customer personas.

2. **Define your research objectives:** Begin by clearly outlining your goals and the purpose of creating customer personas. This step ensures that your research efforts align with your overall marketing strategy.

3. **Conduct internal interviews:** Engage with your internal team, including sales, customer service, and marketing personnel, to gather insights on customer behavior, pain points, and preferences. Compile this data to form a foundation for persona development.

4. **Analyze existing customer data**: Utilize your CRM system, customer surveys, and website analytics to extract relevant information about your existing customer base. Identify common characteristics, patterns, and trends to guide your persona creation process.

5. **Conduct qualitative research:** Plan and execute in-depth interviews, focus groups, or surveys with a sample of your target audience. This primary research helps you understand their motivations, challenges, and aspirations in their own words.

6. **Identify demographic and firmographic attributes**: Segment your audience based on demographic factors such as age, gender, location, and occupation. For B2B businesses, consider firmographic details like industry, company size, and job title.

7. **Explore psychographic characteristics**: Dive deeper into your audience's psychographic traits, including their values, attitudes, lifestyle choices, and interests. Understand their decision-making processes, influences, and media consumption habits.

8. **Uncover pain points and goals**: Identify the problems your customers face and the goals they aspire to achieve. Pinpoint the challenges they encounter, which your products or services can help overcome.

9. **Create fictional personas:** Synthesize the collected data and insights to develop representative customer personas. Give each persona a name, photo, and a detailed description that encompasses their demographics, psychographics, goals, challenges, and preferences.

10. **Validate personas with data**: Use data analysis and market research techniques to verify the accuracy and relevance of your personas. Update and refine them as needed based on the findings.

11. **Utilize personas across marketing efforts**: Incorporate your customer personas into various aspects of your marketing strategy. Tailor your content, messaging, and campaigns to resonate with each persona. Use personas to inform product development, customer experience design, and lead generation strategies.

Finally, once the personas are developed and validated, businesses should utilize them across their marketing efforts. This means tailoring content, messaging, and campaigns to resonate with each persona. Personas should inform various aspects of marketing, including product development, customer experience design, and lead generation strategies.

By following these steps, businesses can create customer personas that facilitate a better understanding of their target audience and help forge stronger connections with them.

Now let's look at a few examples of developing buyer personas for a SaaS company:

Buyer Persona: Marketing Mary

Demographics: Female, aged 30-40, works as a marketing manager in a medium-sized technology company.

Pain Points: Struggles with lead generation, lacks a centralized marketing automation tool, and seeks solutions to streamline campaign management.

Goals: Increase website traffic, generate qualified leads, and improve marketing ROI.

Buyer Persona: Entrepreneurial Eric

Demographics: Male, aged 25-35, founder of a startup in the e-commerce industry.

Pain Points: Limited marketing budget, seeks cost-effective tools for email marketing and social media management, desires scalability and ease of use.

Goals: Build brand awareness, acquire new customers, and drive revenue growth.

By creating detailed buyer personas based on research, surveys, and data analysis, you gain insights into your target customers' needs and preferences, enabling you to tailor your marketing strategies accordingly.

However, please remember that any customer personas can fail for various reasons. Firstly, insufficient or inaccurate research can lead to personas that do not accurately represent the target audience. Overgeneralization, based on stereotypes or assumptions, can result in personas that do not capture the diversity of customer preferences and behaviours.

Neglecting to update personas with evolving customer insights can render them outdated and less effective. If personas are not grounded in real data and lack validation, they may fail to resonate with the target audience. Limited implementation of personas in marketing strategies can also diminish their impact. Lastly, failing to recognize individuality within persona groups can lead to generalized approaches that do not connect with customers on a personal level.

To mitigate these issues, thorough research, data validation, regular updates, effective implementation, and consideration of individual variations are essential for successful customer personas.

3.3 Creating a Unique Value Proposition:

A unique value proposition (UVP) communicates the unique benefits and value your SaaS product offers to customers. It differentiates your product from competitors and convinces potential customers to choose your solution. Consider the following components when creating your UVP:

a) **Target Customer**: Clearly define your target customers and address their specific pain points. For example, if your SaaS product is project management software, your UVP could be tailored towards small businesses seeking streamlined project collaboration.

b) **Key Benefits:** Highlight the primary benefits and features that solve your customers' pain points. For instance, emphasize how your project management software simplifies task assignment, improves team communication, and increases productivity.

c) **Differentiation:** Identify what sets your SaaS product apart from competitors. It could be unique features, a user-friendly interface, excellent customer support, or integrations with popular platforms.

Real-world example: Dropbox

- **Target Customer:** Individuals and businesses needing secure file storage and seamless collaboration.

- **Key Benefits:** Access files from anywhere, easy file sharing and collaboration, automatic backup, and version control.

- **Differentiation:** Simple and intuitive user interface, cross-platform compatibility, and seamless integration with popular productivity tools.

When finding a unique value proposition (UVP), there are some common mistakes that people make. Here are a few of them and suggestions on how to avoid them:

- **Lack of Customer Research:** One common mistake is not conducting thorough customer research to understand their pain points, needs, and preferences. To avoid this, invest time in gathering insights through surveys, interviews, and market research. Engage with your target audience to gain a deep understanding of their challenges and aspirations.

- **Focusing on Features Instead of Benefits**: Another mistake is emphasizing product features rather than the benefits they provide to customers. Instead, shift the focus to how your product solves their problems and fulfills their needs. Clearly communicate the value and outcomes your solution delivers.

- **Ignoring Competitor Analysis:** Neglecting to research and analyze your competitors can hinder your ability to differentiate your UVP. Take the time to understand what your competitors are offering and identify gaps or areas where you can excel. Highlight the unique aspects that set your product apart from the competition.

- **Lack of Clarity and Conciseness:** A common mistake is having a UVP that is unclear or too lengthy. Your UVP should be concise, easily understandable, and compelling. Avoid jargon or complex language. Craft a clear and impactful statement that captures the essence of what you offer and why it matters to your target audience.

- **Not Testing and Iterating**: Failing to test your UVP with your target audience can be a missed opportunity. Collect feedback and insights from potential customers to refine and improve your messaging. Iterate and adapt based on their responses to ensure your UVP resonates effectively.

To avoid these mistakes, invest time in comprehensive customer research, focus on communicating the benefits rather than features, conduct competitor analysis, ensure clarity and conciseness in your UVP statement, and continuously test and iterate based on customer feedback. By avoiding these common pitfalls, you can develop a compelling UVP that effectively differentiates your product and resonates with your target audience.

By incorporating these components into your SaaS marketing strategy, you can set clear goals, understand your target audience, and communicate your unique value proposition effectively, thereby increasing your chances of success in the competitive SaaS market.

Finally, you would also need an approach to combine all of the above and create a go-to-market plan for your product. Here is my DEFINE framework that has worked well for me.

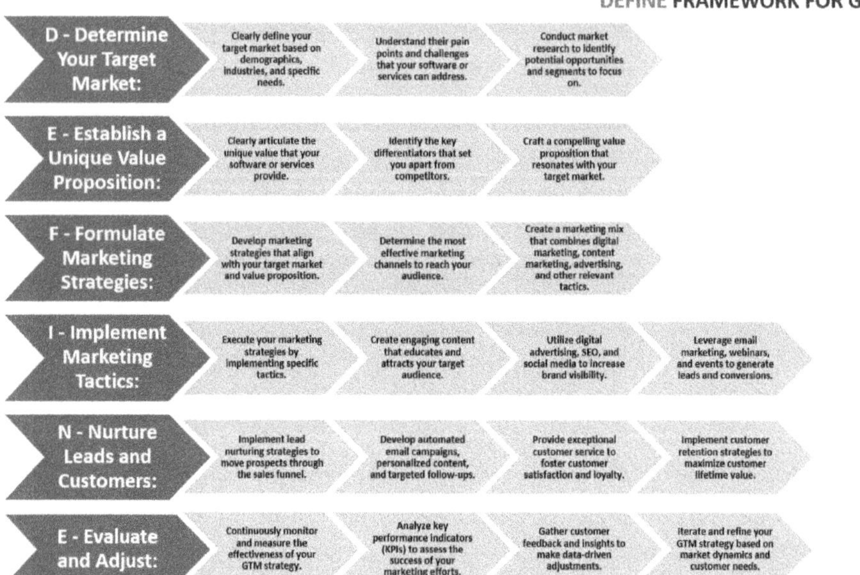

Here's a Go-To-Market (GTM) framework that aligns with the marketing plan for selling both software and services:

3.3.1 DEFINE

D - Determine Your Target Market:

- Clearly define your target market based on demographics, industries, and specific needs.
- Understand their pain points and challenges that your software or services can address.
- Conduct market research to identify potential opportunities and segments to focus on.

E - Establish Unique Value Proposition:

- Clearly articulate the unique value that your software or services provide.

- Identify the key differentiators that set you apart from competitors.
- Craft a compelling value proposition that resonates with your target market.

F - Formulate Marketing Strategies:

- Develop marketing strategies that align with your target market and value proposition.
- Determine the most effective marketing channels to reach your audience.
- Create a marketing mix that combines digital marketing, content marketing, advertising, and other relevant tactics.

I - Implement Marketing Tactics:

- Execute your marketing strategies by implementing specific tactics.
- Create engaging content that educates and attracts your target audience.
- Utilize digital advertising, SEO, and social media to increase brand visibility.
- Leverage email marketing, webinars, and events to generate leads and conversions.

N - Nurture Leads and Customers:

- Implement lead nurturing strategies to move prospects through the sales funnel.
- Develop automated email campaigns, personalized content, and targeted follow-ups.

- Provide exceptional customer service to foster customer satisfaction and loyalty.
- Implement customer retention strategies to maximize customer lifetime value.

E - Evaluate and Adjust:

- Continuously monitor and measure the effectiveness of your GTM strategy.
- Analyze key performance indicators (KPIs) to assess the success of your marketing efforts.
- Gather customer feedback and insights to make data-driven adjustments.
- Iterate and refine your GTM strategy based on market dynamics and customer needs.

By following the DEFINE GTM framework, you can create a structured approach to effectively bring your software or services to the market. It helps you define your target market, establish a unique value proposition, formulate marketing strategies, implement marketing tactics, nurture leads and customers, and continuously evaluate and adjust your GTM approach.

Chapter 4

BUILDING YOUR SAAS BRAND

In this chapter, we will delve into the importance of building a strong brand for your SaaS business. A well-crafted brand helps you establish a unique identity, connect with your target audience, and differentiate yourself in a competitive market. We will explore the significance of branding in SaaS marketing, how to craft a compelling brand story and messaging, and the elements of designing a memorable brand identity. Let's get started!

4.1 The Importance of Branding in SaaS Marketing

Branding plays a crucial role in SaaS marketing, especially considering the ever-growing competition in the industry. It helps shape the perception of your business in the minds of your target customers, going beyond a mere logo or visual design. A strong brand encompasses the overall experience and emotional connection your customers have with your SaaS product, making it vital for long-term success.

Establishing a strong brand is beneficial in several ways. It builds trust, credibility, and loyalty among customers, setting your SaaS product apart from competitors. A well-established brand can command higher prices, attract a loyal customer base, and drive customer referrals, contributing to sustainable growth.

To illustrate the significance of branding in SaaS marketing, let's look at the success stories of prominent SaaS companies over the years.

Consider the case of Salesforce, a pioneer in the SaaS industry. Since its inception in 1999, Salesforce has not only developed outstanding cloud-based customer relationship management (CRM) solutions but has also cultivated a strong brand. It has become a global leader in CRM, with a market capitalization in the tens of billions of dollars. Salesforce's brand is synonymous with reliable and innovative CRM solutions, instilling trust and credibility among its vast customer base.

Another notable example is Slack, which was founded in 2013. Slack has positioned itself as a collaborative and efficient communication platform, emphasizing simplicity and productivity. By creating a strong brand experience, ***Slack has gained widespread popularity and was acquired by Salesforce in 2020 for over $27 billion.*** The brand has become an integral part of many organizations' daily operations, reflecting the power of effective branding.

Canva, a user-friendly and empowering design tool, serves as another compelling illustration. Established in 2012, Canva has not only developed a feature-rich platform but has also built a brand that resonates with its target audience. By offering a seamless design experience and empowering users with creative tools, Canva has become synonymous with accessible and enjoyable design. Its well-crafted brand has contributed to its rapid growth and widespread adoption.

These examples highlight how successful SaaS companies have not only created exceptional products but also cultivated strong brands that resonate with their target audience. By emphasizing the overall brand experience, these companies have established themselves as industry leaders, attracting loyal customers and driving long-term success.

4.2 Crafting a Compelling Brand Story and Messaging

Crafting a compelling brand story and messaging is crucial for both Indian and international IT companies operating in the competitive landscape of the industry. By examining examples from both Indian and international brands, we can understand the significance of these elements in establishing a strong brand presence and resonating with the target audience.

Infosys, headquartered in Bangalore, has successfully built a brand story around delivering business value through innovation and digital transformation. The company's narrative highlights its commitment to helping clients navigate the digital age and drive sustainable growth. This brand story positions Infosys as a trusted partner in clients' success, while the brand message, "Navigate your digital future," reflects the company's dedication to guiding businesses through their digital transformation journey.

Another example is Zoho Corporation, based in Chennai, India, which has established itself as a leading SaaS company offering a suite of cloud-based business software. The brand story of Zoho revolves around empowering businesses of all sizes **with comprehensive and affordable software solutions**. Zoho's brand message emphasizes its commitment to providing accessible and user-friendly SaaS products to help businesses streamline their operations and drive growth.

One of the most popular examples is Apple, a renowned global IT brand, which has crafted a brand story focused on innovation, design, and simplicity. Apple's narrative revolves around inspiring individuals to think differently and embrace the power of technology.

The brand message, **"Think Different,"** encourages people to challenge the status quo, be innovative, and think outside the box. Apple's brand story and messaging have created a strong emotional connection with its audience, driving customer loyalty and setting the brand apart.

However, not beats Slack which is now a widely recognized SaaS brand, offers a collaboration platform that has transformed the way teams communicate and work together. The brand story of Slack centers around promoting efficiency, productivity, and seamless collaboration. By emphasizing a user-friendly interface and integrations with various productivity tools, Slack has created a brand experience that resonates with its target audience.

When crafting a brand story, both Indian and international IT companies should consider the journey that led to the creation of their SaaS product. Reflect on the inspiration, challenges, and solutions developed to address customer needs.

This approach humanizes the brand, making it relatable and memorable to the target audience. For instance, Indian IT giant Wipro focuses its brand story on driving business agility and delivering technology-led solutions, emphasizing its adaptability to changing market needs.

In addition to the brand story, brand messaging plays a vital role in capturing the attention of the target audience. It should be clear, concise, and consistent across all communication channels. Develop key messages that effectively convey the unique value and benefits of the SaaS product, addressing the pain points of the target customers. This approach applies to both Indian and international brands, such as TCS, which emphasizes its commitment to delivering measurable business outcomes for its clients through the brand message, **"Experience certainty."**

By crafting a compelling brand story and messaging, both Indian and international IT companies can differentiate themselves in the competitive landscape. These elements allow them to establish meaningful connections with the target audience, fostering loyalty and long-term relationships. Whether it's an Indian brand like Infosys or an international brand like Apple, showcasing the value and impact of the SaaS product through a well-crafted brand story and messaging is essential in positioning the brand, driving customer engagement, and standing out in the IT industry.

4.3 Designing a Memorable Brand Identity

Your brand identity encompasses the visual elements that represent your SaaS business, such as your logo, color palette, typography, and overall design aesthetic. It should align with your brand story and messaging, reinforcing the desired perception of your brand.

Designing a memorable brand identity is crucial for your SaaS business as it encompasses the visual elements that represent your brand, such as the logo, color palette, typography, and overall design aesthetic. It is essential to ensure that your brand identity aligns with your brand story and messaging, reinforcing the desired perception of your brand.

Investing in professional design is key to creating a cohesive and visually appealing brand identity. Your logo should be distinctive and easily recognizable, serving as a visual symbol of your brand. The color palette and typography choices should evoke the desired emotions and reflect your brand's personality. Consistency in design across all touchpoints, including your website, marketing materials, and social media profiles, is crucial for building a strong and recognizable brand.

A great example of a well-designed brand identity is Dropbox.

Their logo is simple, clean, and instantly recognizable, representing their focus on simplicity and ease of use. The choice of blue as their primary color conveys trust and reliability. The overall design aesthetic is minimalistic and user-friendly, reflecting their brand values and commitment to a seamless user experience.

By designing a memorable brand identity, you enhance brand recognition and create a visual representation that reinforces your brand story and messaging. Consistency in design across all platforms and touchpoints helps create a cohesive brand experience for your customers, establishing trust and loyalty.

Here are 20 examples of SaaS brands with their brand stories, taglines, and marketing stories:

1. **Salesforce:**

    - **Brand Story:** Salesforce revolutionized customer relationship management (CRM) with their cloud-based solutions, empowering businesses to better engage with their customers.
    - **Tagline:** "The World's #1 CRM"
    - **Marketing Story:** Salesforce helps businesses build strong customer relationships, drive sales, and deliver exceptional experiences through their comprehensive CRM platform.

2. **HubSpot:**
    - **Brand Story:** HubSpot provides inbound marketing and sales software, helping businesses attract, engage, and delight customers by transforming their marketing strategies.
    - **Tagline:** "Grow better"
    - **Marketing Story:** HubSpot offers a suite of tools that enable businesses to create and optimize content, generate leads, and deliver personalized experiences to drive growth.

3. **Adobe:**
    - **Brand Story:** Adobe has been at the forefront of digital creativity, offering industry-leading software solutions for designers, photographers, and marketers.
    - **Tagline:** "Changing the world through digital experiences"
    - **Marketing Story:** Adobe empowers creative professionals and marketers with tools to design stunning visuals, deliver engaging content, and create memorable digital experiences.

4. **Slack:**
    - **Brand Story:** Slack is a team collaboration platform that replaces email and enables seamless communication and file sharing among teams.
    - **Tagline:** "Where teams work together"
    - **Marketing Story:** Slack simplifies teamwork by bringing all communication, collaboration, and integrations into one central hub, making work more productive and enjoyable.

5. **Zoom:**
    - **Brand Story:** Zoom emerged as a leading video communications platform, providing reliable and high-quality video conferencing experiences for remote meetings and virtual collaboration.

   - **Tagline:** "Delivering happiness through video communications"
   - **Marketing Story:** Zoom enables teams and individuals to connect, collaborate, and communicate effectively through crystal-clear video and audio, creating seamless virtual meeting experiences.

6. **Monday.com:**
   - **Brand Story:** Monday.com offers a customizable work operating system that helps teams manage projects, workflows, and tasks efficiently.
   - **Tagline:** "Work the way that works for you"
   - **Marketing Story:** Monday.com provides a visual and collaborative platform where teams can plan, track progress, and achieve their goals, fostering transparency and productivity.

7. **Dropbox:**
   - **Brand Story:** Dropbox provides secure file storage and sharing solutions, allowing individuals and businesses to access their files from anywhere.
   - **Tagline:** "Your files, anywhere"
   - **Marketing Story:** Dropbox simplifies file management and collaboration, enabling users to store, share, and collaborate on documents seamlessly across devices and platforms.

8. **Canva:**
   - **Brand Story:** Canva is a user-friendly graphic design platform that empowers individuals and businesses to create professional-quality designs easily.
   - **Tagline:** "Empowering the world to design"
   - **Marketing Story:** Canva offers a wide range of customizable templates, intuitive design tools, and an extensive library of visuals to help anyone create beautiful designs effortlessly.

9. **Shopify:**
   - **Brand Story:** Shopify is a leading e-commerce platform that empowers entrepreneurs and businesses to build and manage online stores.
   - **Tagline:** "The future of commerce"
   - **Marketing Story:** Shopify provides a comprehensive suite of tools and services, making it easy for businesses to start, grow, and scale their online stores and reach customers globally.

10. **Mailchimp:**
    - **Brand Story:** Mailchimp is an all-in-one marketing platform that enables businesses to create, automate, and send targeted email campaigns to engage their audience.
    - **Tagline:** "Built for growing businesses"
    - **Marketing Story:** Mailchimp helps businesses build meaningful connections with their audience through email marketing, automation, and data-driven insights, driving growth and customer loyalty.

11. **Zendesk:**
    - **Brand Story:** Zendesk offers customer service and engagement software, empowering businesses to deliver exceptional support experiences and build strong customer relationships.
    - **Tagline:** "Your customers deserve better"
    - **Marketing Story:** Zendesk provides a unified platform that enables businesses to listen, respond, and engage with customers across multiple channels, delivering personalized and efficient support.

12. **Trello:**
    - **Brand Story:** Trello is a visual collaboration tool that helps individuals and teams organize and prioritize tasks, projects, and workflows.

- **Tagline:** "Get more done"
- **Marketing Story:** Trello simplifies task management and collaboration, allowing users to visualize their work, streamline workflows, and achieve greater productivity and efficiency.

13. **Intercom:**
    - **Brand Story:** Intercom is a customer messaging platform that facilitates personalized, real-time communication between businesses and their customers.
    - **Tagline:** "Make business personal"
    - **Marketing Story:** Intercom helps businesses create meaningful conversations, engage customers at the right moments, and build long-lasting relationships through personalized messaging.

14. **QuickBooks:**
    - **Brand Story:** QuickBooks is an accounting software designed to simplify financial management for small businesses and self-employed professionals.
    - **Tagline:** "Backing you"
    - **Marketing Story:** QuickBooks provides easy-to-use tools for invoicing, expense tracking, payroll, and reporting, empowering businesses to manage their finances with confidence.

15. **Slack:**
    - **Brand Story:** Slack is a team collaboration platform that replaces email and enables seamless communication and file sharing among teams.
    - **Tagline:** "Where teams work together"
    - **Marketing Story:** Slack simplifies teamwork by bringing all communication, collaboration, and integrations into one central hub, making work more productive and enjoyable.

16. **Google Workspace:**
    - **Brand Story:** Google Workspace (formerly G Suite) offers a suite of productivity tools including Gmail, Drive, Docs, and more, designed for seamless collaboration and communication.
    - **Tagline:** "Get more done with Google Workspace"
    - **Marketing Story:** Google Workspace provides a comprehensive set of cloud-based tools that facilitate collaboration, productivity, and communication, enabling teams to work together effectively.
17. **Wix:**
    - **Brand Story:** Wix is a leading website builder that allows individuals and businesses to create professional websites without coding knowledge.
    - **Tagline:** "Create your own professional website"
    - **Marketing Story:** Wix provides an intuitive drag-and-drop interface, customizable templates, and a wide range of features to help users build stunning websites and establish their online presence.
18. **Atlassian:**
    - **Brand Story:** Atlassian develops collaboration and productivity software, including Jira, Confluence, and Trello, to empower teams to work together effectively.
    - **Tagline:** "Unleash the potential of every team"
    - **Marketing Story:** Atlassian's suite of tools enables teams to plan, track, and deliver projects, foster knowledge sharing, and enhance collaboration, driving success and innovation.
19. **Evernote:**
    - **Brand Story:** Evernote is a note-taking app that helps individuals capture, organize, and access information across devices to enhance productivity and creativity.

- **Tagline:** "Remember everything"
- **Marketing Story:** Evernote allows users to store ideas, notes, and documents in one place, enabling seamless organization and easy retrieval, resulting in increased efficiency and inspiration.

20. **Asana:**
    - **Brand Story:** Asana is a project management platform that enables teams to plan, track, and manage their work and projects collaboratively.
    - **Tagline:** "Move work forward"
    - **Marketing Story:** Asana helps teams stay organized, prioritize tasks, and achieve their goals by providing a centralized platform that fosters transparency, accountability, and effective collaboration.

These SaaS brands have crafted compelling brand stories, taglines, and marketing narratives that highlight their unique value propositions and resonate with their target audiences, positioning them as leaders in their respective industries.

To build a successful SaaS marketing story, follow these steps commonly followed by successful brands:

i. **Understand your target audience:** Identify your ideal customers and gain a deep understanding of their needs, pain points, and goals. This knowledge will shape your marketing story and ensure it resonates with your audience.

ii. **Define your unique value proposition:** Clearly articulate the unique value that your SaaS product offers to customers. Highlight how it solves their problems, improves efficiency, or delivers specific benefits that differentiate you from competitors.

iii. **Craft a compelling narrative:** Develop a captivating story that showcases how your SaaS product transforms the lives or businesses of your customers. Focus on real-world examples, use cases, or success stories that demonstrate the positive impact of your solution.

iv. **Use clear and concise messaging**: Keep your marketing story concise, avoiding jargon or technical language that may confuse your audience. Use simple and compelling language to communicate the key benefits and outcomes of using your SaaS product.

v. **Showcase social proof:** Incorporate social proof elements such as customer testimonials, case studies, or reviews to build trust and credibility. Demonstrate how your SaaS product has helped existing customers achieve their goals and solve their challenges.

vi. **Leverage storytelling formats:** Utilize various storytelling formats to engage your audience effectively. This could include blog posts, videos, webinars, podcasts, or interactive content that brings your marketing story to life and creates an emotional connection with your audience.

vii. **Align with customer aspirations:** Position your SaaS product as a solution that helps customers achieve their aspirations or overcome their biggest challenges. Connect your marketing story to their goals, dreams, or desires, making it compelling and relatable.

viii. **Consistency across channels:** Ensure your marketing story is consistent across all marketing channels and touchpoints. Whether it's your website, social media, email campaigns, or advertisements, maintain a cohesive narrative that reinforces your value proposition.

ix. **Continuously refine and evolve:** Regularly evaluate the effectiveness of your marketing story and make adjustments based on customer feedback, market trends, or evolving needs. Continuously refine your messaging to stay relevant and compelling.

x. **Engage with customers:** Foster a strong relationship with your customers by actively engaging with them through social media, forums, or events.

Listen to their feedback, address their concerns, and incorporate their experiences into your marketing story.

By following these steps, you can build a compelling and effective SaaS marketing story that resonates with your target audience, differentiates your brand, and drives customer engagement and growth.

In summary, building a strong brand is essential for the success of your SaaS marketing efforts. It allows you to establish a unique identity, build trust with your target audience, and differentiate your SaaS offering. By crafting a compelling brand story, messaging, and designing a memorable brand identity, you can create a lasting impression and attract loyal customers.

In the next chapter, we will explore the significance of creating a comprehensive content marketing plan for your SaaS business. Stay tuned to learn how to develop a strategy to produce high-quality content, leverage SEO techniques, and increase visibility.

Notes

Chapter 5

CREATING A CONTENT MARKETING PLAN

In this chapter, we will dive into the world of content marketing and explore how it can fuel the success of your SaaS business. A well-crafted content marketing plan helps you attract and engage your target audience, establish thought leadership, and drive organic traffic to your SaaS product. We will discuss the process of developing a content strategy for SaaS products, producing high-quality content across various formats, and leveraging SEO techniques to increase visibility. Let's begin!

5.1 Developing a Content Strategy for SaaS Products

A content strategy is a roadmap that outlines the types of content you will create, the platforms you will utilize, and the goals you aim to achieve. It serves as a guiding framework to ensure your content efforts align with your overall marketing objectives.

To develop an effective content strategy for your SaaS product, start by understanding your target audience's pain points, interests, and preferences. Consider the stage of the buyer's journey they are in and the type of content that will resonate with them at each stage.

For example, if your SaaS product is project management software, your target audience might include project managers, team leaders, and small business owners. At the awareness stage, you can create blog posts or videos highlighting common project management challenges. At the consideration stage, you might produce comparison guides or case studies that showcase the benefits of your software. Finally, at the decision stage, you can offer free trials, demos, or customer testimonials to encourage sign-ups.

Here's an overview of the content strategies of the top 20 SaaS companies, along with examples of their content initiatives:

1. **Salesforce:**
   - **Content Strategy:** Salesforce focuses on thought leadership and educational content that empowers businesses to succeed with CRM and digital transformation.
   - **Example:** Salesforce's blog features industry insights, customer success stories, and expert advice on sales, marketing, customer service, and technology trends.
2. **HubSpot:**
   - **Content Strategy:** HubSpot is renowned for its inbound marketing expertise, providing educational content on various aspects of marketing, sales, and customer service.
   - **Example:** HubSpot Academy offers free online courses and certifications, empowering marketers with practical skills and knowledge.
3. **Adobe:**
   - **Content Strategy:** Adobe creates content that inspires and educates creatives and marketers, showcasing the power of their design and marketing software.
   - **Example:** Adobe's YouTube channel features tutorials, creative challenges, and inspiring videos that demonstrate the possibilities of their tools.

4. **Slack:**

   - **Content Strategy:** Slack focuses on content that explores workplace collaboration, productivity, and remote work, offering tips and insights for teams.
   - **Example:** Slack's blog covers topics like team communication, remote work best practices, and productivity tips to help teams work effectively.

5. **Zoom:**

   - **Content Strategy:** Zoom provides educational content on video conferencing, remote collaboration, and virtual events, demonstrating the benefits of their platform.
   - **Example:** Zoom's resource center offers guides, webinars, and blog articles that provide best practices and tips for hosting successful virtual meetings.

6. **Monday.com:**

   - **Content Strategy:** Monday.com creates content that emphasizes productivity, project management, and team collaboration to help businesses streamline their workflows.
   - **Example:** Monday.com's blog features articles on team management, project planning, and productivity hacks, providing actionable insights for teams.

7. **Dropbox:**

   - **Content Strategy:** Dropbox focuses on content that explores file collaboration, remote work, and data security, highlighting the value of its cloud storage platform.
   - **Example:** Dropbox's blog covers topics like remote work tips, data privacy, and collaboration strategies to help businesses work smarter and securely.

8. **Canva:**
    - **Content Strategy:** Canva offers content that inspires creativity, provides design tips, and showcases real-world use cases for their graphic design platform.
    - **Example:** Canva's Design School features tutorials, design inspiration, and resources to help users create stunning visuals and graphics.

9. **Shopify:**
    - **Content Strategy:** Shopify creates content that helps entrepreneurs and businesses succeed in e-commerce, providing guidance on starting, managing, and growing online stores.
    - **Example:** Shopify's blog offers insights on marketing strategies, store optimization, and success stories to inspire and educate online merchants. They have also started producing industry blog content, podcasts, and video series on topics like starting an online store, e-commerce SEO, and social media marketing for businesses.

10. **Mailchimp:**
    - **Content Strategy:** Mailchimp focuses on content that educates marketers and small businesses on email marketing best practices, automation, and audience engagement.
    - **Example:** Mailchimp's content includes guides, case studies, list segmentation, and A/B testing for email marketing and marketing resources to help users optimize their email campaigns and grow their audience.

By mapping out your content strategy based on your target audience's needs and the buyer's journey, you can deliver relevant and valuable content that guides potential customers toward choosing your SaaS product.

5.2 Producing High-Quality Content

Creating high-quality content is key to capturing the attention and engagement of your target audience. High-quality content is informative, well researched, and provides value to the reader.

Consider the different content formats that can resonate with your audience, such as blog posts, eBooks, videos, podcasts, infographics, or webinars. Each format has its unique strengths, and a diverse content mix can cater to various learning preferences.

When it comes to SaaS marketing content, several factors contribute to its quality and effectiveness. Here are key factors that determine the quality of SaaS marketing content:

1. **Alignment with Target Audience:** Quality SaaS marketing content should resonate with the specific target audience. It should address their pain points, challenges, and aspirations, showcasing how the SaaS solution can provide value and solve their problems.

2. **Clear Value Proposition**: Effective SaaS marketing content clearly communicates the unique value proposition (UVP) of the product or service. It highlights the key benefits and features that differentiate it from competitors and emphasizes how it can meet the target audience's needs.

3. **Educational and Informative:** High-quality SaaS marketing content educates and informs the target audience. It provides valuable insights, industry trends, best practices, and actionable tips that demonstrate thought leadership and help the audience make informed decisions.

4. **Engaging and Persuasive:** Quality SaaS marketing content captivates the audience through an engaging writing style, compelling storytelling, and persuasive messaging. It uses persuasive techniques to convince the audience of the value and benefits of the SaaS solution.

5. **Problem-Solution Focus:** Effective SaaS marketing content focuses on the problems and challenges faced by the target audience and highlights how

the SaaS solution can provide a viable and effective solution. It shows a deep understanding of the audience's pain points and positions the SaaS product as the answer.

6. **Clear Call-to-Action (CTA):** High-quality SaaS marketing content includes clear and compelling calls-to-action. It guides the audience toward the desired action, whether it's signing up for a free trial, scheduling a demo, or making a purchase.

7. **Data-Driven:** Quality SaaS marketing content utilizes data and statistics to support claims, demonstrate the effectiveness of the solution, and build trust with the audience. It provides evidence-backed insights and success stories to showcase real-world results.

8. **Customer-Centric:** Effective SaaS marketing content focuses on the customer's needs, desires, and success. It highlights customer testimonials, case studies, and use cases to demonstrate how the SaaS solution has positively impacted existing customers.

9. **Consistency and Branding:** High-quality SaaS marketing content maintains consistency in branding, tone of voice, and messaging across different channels and content formats. It reflects the brand's values, personality, and positioning to establish a strong brand identity.

10. **Measurable Goals and Analytics**: Quality SaaS marketing content is tied to measurable goals and objectives. It leverages analytics and tracking to evaluate the effectiveness of content, make data-driven optimizations, and continuously improve marketing strategies.

By considering these factors, SaaS marketers can develop high-quality content that engages the target audience, communicates the value proposition effectively, and drives conversions and customer acquisition.

For example, suppose your SaaS product is a social media management tool. In that case, you can create blog posts on strategies for increasing organic reach on different platforms or produce tutorial videos demonstrating how to schedule and analyze social media posts effectively.

5.3 Understanding Marketing Channels

When it comes to marketing a Software as a Service (SaaS) product, reaching your target audience and effectively promoting your offering is essential for success. Fortunately, there are numerous channels available to help you achieve these goals. By utilizing a combination of digital and traditional marketing strategies, you can maximize your product's visibility and engage with potential customers in meaningful ways. In this article, we will explore some common marketing channels for SaaS products, providing you with valuable insights to craft a comprehensive marketing strategy tailored to your specific needs

<u>Try to have a Moon chart to know the degree to which you will engage with each of them</u>

Details around each of these channels is given below;

1. **Website:** Your website is a crucial marketing channel for your SaaS product. Optimize it for search engines (SEO) to increase organic traffic, create compelling landing pages, and provide detailed information about your product, features, pricing, and benefits. Include demo videos, testimonials, and case studies to showcase your value proposition.

2. **Content Marketing:** Develop a content marketing strategy to attract and engage your target audience. Create informative and valuable content such as blog posts, white papers, e-books, and tutorials that address pain points, industry trends, and solutions related to your SaaS product. Distribute your content through your blog, social media, email newsletters, and industry publications.

3. **Paid Advertising:** Utilize pay-per-click (PPC) advertising platforms like Google Ads, Bing Ads, or social media advertising (Facebook Ads, LinkedIn Ads, Twitter Ads) to reach a wider audience. Target specific keywords, demographics, and interests to maximize your ad visibility and conversions. Retargeting campaigns can also be effective in reminding potential customers about your product.

4. **Social Media:** Leverage social media platforms to build brand awareness, engage with your audience, and promote your SaaS product. Identify the platforms most relevant to your target audience and create compelling content, share updates, run contests, and participate in industry conversations. LinkedIn, Twitter, Facebook, and YouTube are popular options.

5. **Influencer Marketing:** Collaborate with influencers or industry experts who have a significant following in your target market. They can promote your SaaS product through reviews, sponsored content, or by sharing their positive experiences. This can help you reach a wider audience and build credibility.

6. **Email Marketing:** Build an email list of interested prospects and existing customers. Use email marketing campaigns to nurture leads, share product updates, announce new features, and provide valuable content. Segment your email list to send personalized and targeted messages to improve engagement and conversions.

7. **Partnerships and Affiliates:** Identify potential partners, such as complementary SaaS providers or industry associations, and explore collaboration opportunities. This can include cross-promotion, joint

webinars, guest blogging, or offering affiliate programs where others earn a commission for referring customers to your product.

8. **Events and Webinars:** Participate in relevant industry events, trade shows, conferences, or host your own webinars to showcase your SaaS product. These platforms provide opportunities to engage directly with potential customers, demonstrate your product's value, and build relationships.

Crafting a successful marketing strategy for your SaaS product requires a thoughtful approach that integrates multiple channels to reach and engage your target audience. By optimizing your website, leveraging content marketing, utilizing paid advertising, harnessing the power of social media, leveraging influencer marketing, implementing email campaigns, exploring partnerships and affiliates, and participating in events and webinars, you can establish a strong brand presence and effectively showcase your SaaS product's value. Remember to continuously track and analyze your marketing efforts, allowing you to refine your strategy and optimize your approach over time. With a well-rounded and adaptable marketing plan, you can increase your product's visibility, attract new customers, and drive the growth and success of your SaaS business.

5.4 Leveraging SEO Techniques to Increase Visibility

Search Engine Optimization (SEO) is crucial for increasing the visibility of your content and driving organic traffic to your SaaS product. By optimizing your content for relevant keywords and improving your website's search engine rankings, you can attract potential customers who are actively searching for solutions in your industry.

Start by conducting keyword research to identify the terms and phrases your target audience is using when searching for information related to your SaaS product. Incorporate these keywords strategically throughout your content, including in titles, headings, meta descriptions, and body text. However, remember to prioritize user experience and avoid keyword stuffing, as search engines value content that provides value to readers.

In addition to keyword optimization, focus on creating valuable and shareable content that naturally attracts backlinks from reputable websites. Backlinks act as endorsements for your content, signalling to search engines that your content is authoritative and relevant.

Furthermore, optimize technical aspects of your website, such as site speed, mobile responsiveness, and user-friendly navigation, as these factors also contribute to improved search engine rankings.

Now let's look at some of the frequent mistakes SaaS companies make in SEO or SEM efforts, along with quick-fix against each:

- **Lack of Keyword Research**: Many SaaS companies fail to conduct thorough keyword research, resulting in poor visibility and targeting. Solution: Perform keyword research to identify relevant keywords and incorporate them strategically into website content, metadata, and ad campaigns.

- **Neglecting On-Page Optimization:** Ignoring on-page SEO elements like title tags, meta descriptions, and header tags can hinder search engine rankings. Solution: Optimize on-page elements to align with target keywords, improve crawlability, and enhance user experience.

- **Thin or Duplicate Content:** Having thin or duplicate content can negatively impact search rankings and user engagement. Solution: Create high-quality, unique, and informative content that provides value to users. Remove or rewrite duplicate content to avoid penalties.

- **Neglecting Mobile Optimization**: Failing to optimize websites and ads for mobile devices can lead to poor user experiences and lower search rankings. Solution: Implement responsive design, optimize page speed, and ensure mobile-friendly usability for better mobile performance.

- **Poor Link Building Strategies:** Building low-quality or spammy backlinks can harm search rankings and credibility. Solution: Focus on earning high-quality, authoritative backlinks through guest blogging, content partnerships, influencer outreach, and creating valuable content that naturally attracts links.

- **Ineffective Local SEO:** Neglecting local SEO efforts can hinder visibility for SaaS companies targeting specific geographic areas. Solution: Optimize local listings, create location-specific content, and encourage customer reviews to improve local search rankings.

- **Ignoring Technical SEO:** Neglecting technical SEO aspects like site structure, crawlability, and XML sitemaps can hinder search engine visibility. Solution: Conduct regular technical SEO audits, fix broken links, improve site speed, and ensure proper indexing and crawling.

- **Poor Landing Page Optimization:** Having poorly optimized landing pages can result in low conversion rates and wasted ad spend. Solution: Test and optimize landing pages for better user experience, relevancy, and conversion rates. Use tools like heatmaps and A/B testing to improve performance.

- **Inadequate Analytics and Tracking:** Failing to set up proper analytics and tracking mechanisms makes it difficult to measure the effectiveness of SEO or SEM efforts. Solution: Implement tools like Google Analytics and set up conversion tracking to monitor key metrics and make data-driven decisions.

- **Lack of Continuous Monitoring and Optimization:** Not monitoring SEO or SEM campaigns regularly and making necessary adjustments can lead to missed opportunities. Solution: Monitor performance regularly, analyze data, and make iterative optimizations to improve rankings, traffic, and conversions.

By avoiding these mistakes and implementing the suggested solutions, SaaS companies can enhance their SEO and SEM strategies, improve search visibility, increase organic traffic, and drive more qualified leads to their products or services. It's essential to stay updated with the latest SEO and SEM practices, algorithms, and industry trends to maintain a competitive advantage in the digital landscape.

In summary, a well-crafted content marketing plan is essential for the success of your SaaS business. By developing a strategy that aligns with your target audience's needs, producing high-quality content, and leveraging SEO techniques, you can attract, engage, and convert potential customers.

In the next chapter, we will explore the concept of inbound marketing and its role in attracting and nurturing leads for your SaaS product. Stay tuned to learn how to optimize your landing pages, build customer relationships, and drive conversions through inbound marketing strategies.

Chapter 6

IMPLEMENTING INBOUND MARKETING

In this chapter, we will explore the power of inbound marketing in driving lead generation and nurturing customer relationships for your SaaS business. Inbound marketing focuses on attracting, engaging, and delighting customers through valuable content and experiences. We will discuss strategies for attracting and converting leads through inbound marketing, lead nurturing techniques, and optimizing landing pages and conversion funnels. Let's dive in!

6.1 Attracting and Converting Leads through Inbound Marketing

One of the key goals of inbound marketing is to attract qualified leads to your SaaS product. By providing valuable content and experiences, you can position your brand as an industry authority and build trust with your target audience.

However, most of the SaaS companies face challenges in attracting and converting leads through inbound marketing for several reasons:

- **Inadequate Targeting:** One common reason is failing to define a precise target audience for their SaaS product. Without a clear understanding of the ideal customer profile, it becomes difficult to create content that resonates with and attracts the right leads.

- **Weak Value Proposition:** If the SaaS company's value proposition is not clearly articulated or lacks differentiation, it may fail to capture the attention of potential leads. A compelling and unique value proposition is essential for attracting and converting leads through inbound marketing.

- **Lack of Content Strategy:** Inbound marketing relies heavily on content creation, and a lack of a comprehensive content strategy can hinder lead generation efforts. If the SaaS company doesn't produce valuable, relevant, and consistent content that addresses the pain points and interests of their target audience, it may struggle to attract and engage leads.

- **Ineffective Lead Magnets**: Lead magnets, such as e-books, whitepapers, or webinars, are valuable resources used to capture leads' contact information. If the lead magnets offered by the SaaS company are not compelling or fail to address the target audience's needs, it can result in low conversion rates.

- **Poor Landing Page Optimization:** Landing pages play a crucial role in converting leads. If SaaS companies have poorly optimized landing pages that lack clear and persuasive messaging, a strong call-to-action, or an intuitive user experience, they may struggle to convert inbound traffic into leads.

- **Insufficient Lead Nurturing:** Inbound marketing is not just about attracting leads but also nurturing and guiding them through the sales funnel. If the SaaS company fails to implement effective lead nurturing strategies, such as personalized email campaigns, targeted content offers, or marketing automation, leads may become disengaged and fail to convert.

- **Lack of Marketing-Product Alignment:** Successful inbound marketing requires alignment between marketing efforts and the SaaS product itself. If the product does not fulfill the promises made in marketing content or lacks the features and functionalities that prospects expect, it can hinder lead conversion rates.

- **Poor Tracking and Analytics**: Inbound marketing effectiveness relies on tracking and analyzing data to make informed decisions. If the SaaS company fails to track and analyze key metrics, such as website traffic, conversion rates, or lead quality, it becomes challenging to identify areas for improvement and optimize lead generation efforts.

To address these challenges and improve lead generation through inbound marketing, SaaS companies should focus on defining a precise target audience, refining their value proposition, developing a comprehensive content strategy, optimizing landing pages, implementing effective lead nurturing, ensuring marketing-product alignment, and leveraging data for continuous improvement.

Here are some effective strategies for attracting and converting leads through inbound marketing;

- **Content Creation:** Develop informative and engaging content that addresses the pain points and challenges of your target audience. This can include blog posts, eBooks, webinars, or podcasts. By offering valuable insights and solutions, you can capture the attention and interest of potential leads. This can include blog posts, eBooks, webinars, or podcasts. By offering valuable insights and solutions, you can capture the attention and interest of potential leads.

- **Search Engine Optimization (SEO):** Optimize your content for relevant keywords to improve your search engine rankings. This increases the visibility of your content and helps potential leads find your SaaS product when searching for related information. This increases the visibility of your content and helps potential leads find your SaaS product when searching for related information.

- **Social Media Marketing:** Utilize social media platforms to share your content, engage with your audience, and drive traffic to your website. Leverage social media advertising to target specific demographics and expand your reach. Utilize social media management tools like Hootsuite or Buffer to share your content, engage with your audience, and drive traffic to your website. Leverage social media advertising platforms such as Facebook Ads or LinkedIn Ads to target specific demographics and expand your reach.

- **Lead Magnets:** Offer valuable resources or incentives, such as free trials, templates, or exclusive content, in exchange for contact information.

This lets you capture leads and continue nurturing them through targeted marketing efforts. Utilize tools like OptinMonster or Leadpages to create compelling lead magnets such as free trials, templates, or exclusive content. These tools help you capture leads and continue nurturing them through targeted marketing efforts.

In conclusion, attracting and converting leads through inbound marketing is a crucial aspect of SaaS companies' growth strategies. However, several challenges can hinder these efforts. Inadequate targeting, weak value proposition, lack of content strategy, ineffective lead magnets, poor landing page optimization, insufficient lead nurturing, lack of marketing-product alignment, and poor tracking and analytics are common obstacles.

To overcome these challenges and improve lead generation, SaaS companies should focus on defining a precise target audience, refining their value proposition, developing a comprehensive content strategy, optimizing landing pages, implementing effective lead nurturing, ensuring marketing-product alignment, and leveraging data for continuous improvement. Additionally, strategies such as content creation, search engine optimization, social media marketing, and utilizing compelling lead magnets can help attract and convert leads through inbound marketing.

By addressing these factors and executing a well-rounded inbound marketing strategy, SaaS companies can effectively engage and convert leads, driving growth and success in their target markets.

6.2 Lead Nurturing and Building Customer Relationships

Once you have attracted leads to your SaaS product, it's essential to nurture those leads and build strong customer relationships.

SaaS companies face several challenges in lead nurturing and building customer relationships. Some of the top challenges include:

- **Fragmented Customer Data:** SaaS companies often struggle with fragmented customer data across different systems and platforms. Incomplete or disconnected customer data makes it difficult to have a holistic view of the customer and provide personalized nurturing experiences.

- **Lack of Segmentation and Personalization:** Personalization is key to effective lead nurturing, but many SaaS companies struggle with segmenting their leads and delivering tailored content. Without proper segmentation and personalization, lead nurturing efforts can feel generic and fail to resonate with individual leads.

- **Timing and Relevance:** Timing is crucial in lead nurturing, and sending the right message at the right time can significantly impact conversions. SaaS companies may face challenges in determining the optimal timing for sending nurturing emails or content, as well as ensuring the relevance of the content to each lead's stage in the buyer's journey.

- **Scaling Personalization:** As a SaaS company grows and acquires more customers, scaling personalization becomes a challenge. It becomes increasingly difficult to provide personalized experiences and nurture relationships at scale without the right systems and processes in place.

- **Balancing Automation and Human Touch**: Automation is essential for efficient lead nurturing, but finding the right balance between automated processes and the human touch can be challenging. Over-automation can lead to impersonal experiences, while relying too much on human interaction may not be scalable.

- **Integrating Marketing and Sales Efforts:** Lead nurturing requires close collaboration between marketing and sales teams. SaaS companies may face challenges in aligning these two teams and ensuring a smooth handoff of leads from marketing to sales, resulting in a disjointed customer experience.

- **Measuring Effectiveness:** It can be challenging for SaaS companies to accurately measure the effectiveness of their lead nurturing efforts. Attribution and tracking customer interactions across multiple touchpoints can be complex, making it difficult to gauge the impact of lead nurturing activities on conversions and customer relationships.

To overcome these challenges, SaaS companies can focus on improving data management and integration, implementing robust segmentation and personalization strategies, leveraging automation tools while maintaining a human touch, fostering collaboration between marketing and sales teams, and investing in analytics and tracking capabilities to measure the effectiveness of their lead nurturing efforts.

Lead nurturing involves providing relevant and personalized content to guide leads through the buyer's journey and encourage them to take desired actions. Here are some lead nurturing techniques to consider;

- **Email Marketing**: Create targeted email campaigns that deliver valuable content, product updates, and exclusive offers to your leads. Segment your leads based on their interests, behaviors, or stage in the buyer's journey for more personalized communication. Tools like Mailchimp, ActiveCampaign, or Sendinblue can be utilized for effective email marketing.

  Tip: Just be careful not to spam your audience; otherwise, email-id can be restricted and often banned.

- **Marketing Automation**: Utilize marketing automation tools to streamline and automate your lead nurturing processes. This allows you to deliver the right content to the right leads at the right time based on their interactions and behaviors. Tools such as HubSpot, Marketo, or Pardot offer robust marketing automation capabilities.

  Tip: Try to call their sales team for customized packages other than the standard packages that are mentioned on their websites.

- **Personalization:** Tailor your messaging and content to address the specific needs and pain points of each lead. Personalization creates a more engaging and relevant experience, increasing the chances of conversion. Tools like Evergage, Optimizely, or Dynamic Yield provide personalization features to enhance your marketing efforts.

  Tip: Try to have a sample of 30 audiences and check it from the customers' perspective before making it live.

- **Customer Relationship Management (CRM):** Implement a CRM system to track and manage your leads, allowing you to effectively organize and nurture relationships at scale. A CRM system enables you to monitor interactions, track customer preferences, and provide a seamless experience across touchpoints. Popular CRM tools like Salesforce, HubSpot CRM, or Zoho CRM can be utilized for efficient lead management and customer relationship building.

  Tip: Try to have the same DB schema across to avoid any confusion and save it by dates to avoid confusion.

By utilizing these tools, such as Mailchimp, ActiveCampaign, Sendinblue, HubSpot, Marketo, Pardot, Evergage, Optimizely, Dynamic Yield, Salesforce, HubSpot CRM, or Zoho CRM, SaaS companies can effectively implement email marketing, marketing automation, personalization, and CRM strategies to nurture leads and build strong customer relationships.

6.3 Optimizing Landing Pages and Conversion Funnels

To maximize conversions, it's crucial to optimize your landing pages and conversion funnels.

SaaS companies face several challenges when it comes to optimizing landing pages and conversion funnels. Here are some common challenges:

- **Designing an Engaging User Experience:** Creating landing pages that are visually appealing, user-friendly, and optimized for conversion can be a challenge. Balancing aesthetics with functionality and ensuring a seamless user experience requires careful planning and design expertise.

- **Crafting Compelling and Persuasive Copy:** Developing persuasive copy that effectively communicates the value proposition, benefits, and features of the SaaS product can be challenging. Finding the right tone, language, and messaging to engage the target audience and drive conversions is crucial.

- **Implementing Effective Call-to-Action (CTA):** Designing and placing clear and compelling CTAs that prompt visitors to take the desired action can be challenging. Ensuring that the CTA stands out, aligns with the landing page content, and encourages visitors to convert requires careful consideration.

- **Optimizing Conversion Funnels:** Mapping and optimizing the entire conversion funnel, from initial visitor engagement to final conversion, can be complex. Identifying potential bottlenecks, optimizing each step of the funnel, and reducing friction points require constant monitoring and analysis.

- **Conducting A/B Testing and Conversion Rate Optimization:** Implementing effective A/B testing strategies and conversion rate optimization techniques can be challenging. Testing different variations of landing pages, headlines, CTAs, and other elements while accurately measuring and interpreting the results require expertise and resources.

- **Ensuring Mobile Responsiveness:** Creating landing pages that are fully responsive and optimized for mobile devices can be challenging. With the increasing use of mobile devices, SaaS companies need to ensure that their landing pages provide a seamless experience across different screen sizes and resolutions.

- **Balancing SEO and Conversion Optimization:** Striking the right balance between optimizing landing pages for search engines (SEO) and conversion optimization can be a challenge. While it's important to rank well in search results, the landing pages should also be designed to convert visitors into leads or customers.

- **Analyzing and Interpreting Data:** Collecting and analyzing data to gain insights into visitor behavior, conversion rates, and the effectiveness of landing pages can be challenging. Interpreting the data accurately and making data-driven decisions to optimize landing pages and conversion funnels requires expertise in data analysis.

To overcome these challenges, SaaS companies should focus on user-centric design, persuasive copywriting, strategic CTA placement, continuous testing and optimization, mobile responsiveness, collaboration between marketing and design teams, and leveraging data analysis to make informed decisions. Implementing tools and technologies like landing page builders (e.g., Unbounce, Instapage), A/B testing platforms (e.g., Google Optimize, Optimizely), and web analytics tools (e.g., Google Analytics, Hotjar) can also greatly assist in optimizing landing pages and improving conversion funnels.

Now let's understand a landing page where leads land after clicking on a call-to-action or an ad, and it plays a critical role in driving conversions. Here are some tips for optimizing landing pages and conversion funnels:

- **Clear Call-to-Action (CTA)** using tools like Unbounce, Instapage, or Leadpages: Include a clear and compelling CTA that tells leads what action you want them to take. Make it visually prominent and align it with the offer or content on the landing page. Landing page builders like Unbounce, Instapage, or Leadpages offer customizable templates and features for creating effective CTAs.

- **Minimal Form Fields** with tools like Typeform, JotForm, or Wufoo: Keep the form fields on your landing page minimal to reduce friction and increase conversion rates. Only ask for essential information that you need to follow up with leads. Form builders like Typeform, JotForm, or Wufoo provide user-friendly interfaces and options for creating streamlined and responsive forms.

- **Compelling Copy and Design** with tools like Canva, Adobe Creative Cloud, or Figma: Use persuasive copy and engaging design elements to convey the value proposition of your SaaS product. Highlight the benefits, features, and unique selling points that differentiate your product from competitors. Graphic design tools like Canva, Adobe Creative Cloud, or Figma offer templates, graphics, and editing capabilities for creating visually appealing landing page designs.

- **Web A/B Testing** with tools like Google Optimize, Optimizely, or VWO: Continuously test and optimize your landing pages to improve conversion rates. Experiment with different headlines, copy variations,

CTA placements, or design elements to identify what resonates best with your audience. A/B testing tools like Google Optimize, Optimizely, or VWO allow you to create variants of your landing pages and conduct experiments to measure and analyze their performance.

By utilizing these tools such as Unbounce, Instapage, Leadpages, Typeform, JotForm, Wufoo, Canva, Adobe Creative Cloud, Figma, Google Optimize, Optimizely, or VWO, SaaS companies can enhance their landing page optimization efforts, create compelling CTAs, streamline form submissions, design visually appealing pages, and conduct A/B tests for continuous improvement.

Here are a few websites that offer free landing page templates:

- **HubSpot:** HubSpot offers a wide range of free landing page templates that you can customize and use for your marketing campaigns. You can browse and download templates from their template library. Website: https://www.hubspot.com

- **Leadpages:** Leadpages provides a collection of free landing page templates that you can use to create effective landing pages. You can customize the templates using their drag-and-drop editor. Website: https://www.leadpages.com

- **Unbounce:** Unbounce offers a selection of free landing page templates that you can use for your marketing campaigns. Their templates are designed to be mobile-responsive and easy to customize. Website: https://unbounce.com

- **Mailchimp:** Mailchimp provides a range of free landing page templates that you can use to capture leads and promote your products or services. You can customize the templates using their editor. Website: https://www.mailchimp.com

- **Carrd:** Carrd is a simple and intuitive platform that offers free landing page templates. It allows you to create basic landing pages quickly and easily. Website: https://carrd.co

- **Strikingly:** Strikingly offers a selection of free landing page templates that you can use to create professional-looking landing pages. Their templates are responsive and easy to customize. Website: https://www.strikingly.com

- **BootstrapMade:** BootstrapMade provides a collection of free Bootstrap landing page templates. These templates are built on the Bootstrap framework and can be customized to suit your needs. Website: https://bootstrapmade.com

****Remember to review the licensing terms and conditions for each template to ensure they can be used for your specific purposes****

In the next chapter, we will explore how to maximize lead conversion in SaaS marketing by converting Marketing Qualified Leads (MQLs) to Sales Qualified Leads (SQLs). Stay tuned to learn about lead scoring, nurturing techniques, and strategies for optimizing lead conversion.

Notes

Chapter 7

BOOSTING MQL TO SQL CONVERSION RATE IN SAAS MARKETING

In this chapter, we will explore effective strategies to improve the conversion rate from Marketing Qualified Leads (MQLs) to Sales Qualified Leads (SQLs) in the context of SaaS marketing. Converting leads is vital for driving customer growth and maximizing the success of your SaaS business. We will cover the key differences between MQLs and SQLs, the importance of tracking conversion rates, and provide actionable strategies to enhance your MQL to SQL conversion rate. Let's dive in!

7.1 Understanding MQLs and SQLs

To begin, let's clarify the definitions of MQLs and SQLs:

- **Marketing Qualified Lead (MQL):** An MQL represents a potential customer who fits your buyer persona and has been reviewed and confirmed by the marketing team. However, they may not be ready for direct sales engagement.

- **Sales Qualified Lead (SQL)**: An SQL is a prospective customer who exhibits a clear and strong intent to purchase your SaaS product. They are in the final stages of the buying cycle and are ready for direct sales follow-up.

The main distinction between MQLs and SQLs lies in the customer's intent to buy the product. MQLs require further nurturing and engagement from the marketing team, while SQLs are primed for personalized sales interaction.

7.2 Importance of Tracking MQL to SQL Conversion Rate

Tracking the MQL to SQL conversion rate is crucial for evaluating and improving your marketing efforts. By monitoring this conversion rate, you can:

1. Assess the effectiveness of your marketing strategies in generating sales-ready leads.
2. Determine how frequently leads are successfully converted from MQLs to SQLs.
3. Evaluate the performance of your sales team in generating qualified leads.
4. Analyze the performance of your company or teams and identify areas for improvement.
5. Compare your conversion rate with industry benchmarks to gauge your performance.

7.3 Strategies to Boost MQL to SQL Conversion Rate

To improve your MQL to SQL conversion rate, consider implementing the following actionable strategies:

- ✔ **Align Sales and Marketing Teams:** Ensure that your sales and marketing teams work collaboratively and have access to the same data. Eliminate any "dark funnels" where potential customers are lost due to data gaps between teams.

Example: Slack

Slack ensures alignment between their sales and marketing teams by implementing a shared customer relationship management (CRM) system. Both teams have access to the same data, allowing them to collaborate seamlessly and eliminate any data gaps that could lead to potential customer loss.

- ✔ **Set Customer Expectations:** Avoid overpromising in your marketing messaging to prevent a customer service gap. Align your messaging with the actual capabilities of your SaaS product, ensuring customer expectations are realistic.

  Example: Dropbox

  Dropbox aligns their marketing messaging with the actual capabilities of their SaaS product. They focus on delivering clear and realistic messages about their product's features and functionalities, ensuring that customer expectations are accurately set from the start.

- ✔ **Showcase Success Stories:** Create compelling case studies that highlight the successes and benefits experienced by existing customers. These case studies serve as social proof and build trust with potential customers.

  Example: Adobe Experience Cloud

  Adobe Experience Cloud utilizes an ABM strategy to engage with high-value target accounts. They personalize their marketing efforts by creating tailored content and experiences for each target account, demonstrating an understanding of their specific needs and increasing the likelihood of conversion.

- ✔ **Implement Account-Based Marketing (ABM):** Develop an ABM strategy to proactively engage with high-value target accounts. Personalize your marketing efforts to create a tailored buying experience for these accounts, increasing the likelihood of conversion.

Example: Adobe Experience Cloud

Adobe Experience Cloud utilizes an ABM strategy to engage with high-value target accounts. They personalize their marketing efforts by creating tailored content and experiences for each target account, demonstrating an understanding of their specific needs and increasing the likelihood of conversion.

- **Collect Customer Feedback:** Gather feedback from existing customers to gain insights into their motivations and needs. Utilize in-app microsurveys or customer feedback tools to collect valuable data for identifying new potential customers and refining your product or service offerings.

  Example: Airbnb

  Airbnb actively gathers feedback from their users through in-app surveys and customer feedback channels. They leverage this feedback to gain insights into customer motivations and needs, which helps them refine their platform and offerings to better serve both hosts and guests.

- **Create a Follow-up Schedule:** Establish a well-defined follow-up schedule for your sales team to ensure timely and effective engagement with leads. Utilize automation tools to streamline and automate follow-up processes.

  Example: Salesforce Sales Cloud

  Salesforce Sales Cloud enables sales teams to establish a well-defined follow-up schedule through automation tools. They use features like task management and email reminders to ensure timely and effective engagement with leads, improving the chances of conversion.

- **Nurture Leads with Personalized Emails:** Develop personalized email nurturing campaigns to influence customer behavior and drive conversions.

Use contextual email marketing to deliver personalized content, such as demo materials, that align with each lead's needs.

Example: Amazon Web Services (AWS)

AWS develops personalized email nurturing campaigns to engage potential customers. They deliver targeted content, such as case studies and whitepapers, based on the specific needs and interests of each lead. This personalized approach helps drive conversions and encourages further engagement.

- **Encourage Customer Reviews:** Ask satisfied customers for reviews and testimonials to enhance your brand's reputation and drive referrals. Leverage in-app modals or surveys to gather feedback at specific touchpoints in the customer journey.

  Example: Yelp

  Yelp encourages satisfied customers to leave reviews and testimonials on their platform. By leveraging user-generated content and social proof, Yelp enhances their brand's reputation, builds trust with potential customers, and drives referrals to businesses listed on their platform.

- **Conduct Fake Door Testing:** Use fake door testing to gauge customer interest and demand for potential product features before committing to full development. This approach allows you to validate ideas, refine pricing strategies, and identify high-demand features.

  Example: Spotify

  Spotify conducts fake door testing to gauge customer interest and demand for potential features before fully developing them. They test out new features or functionalities with a small subset of users to gather feedback and validate ideas, allowing them to prioritize development efforts effectively.

- **Analyze and Optimize Marketing Campaigns:** Regularly analyze your marketing campaigns to identify weak points and optimize their performance. Evaluate the effectiveness of your sales processes and training to ensure your sales team is equipped to handle leads effectively.

  Example: Google Ads

  Google Ads provides robust analytics and reporting features to help businesses analyze and optimize their marketing campaigns. With data-driven insights, businesses can identify underperforming areas, refine their targeting strategies, and optimize their sales processes to improve lead conversion rates.

These examples demonstrate how real-life companies have implemented the mentioned strategies to align sales and marketing teams, set customer expectations, showcase success stories, implement ABM, collect customer feedback, create follow-up schedules; nurture leads with personalized emails, encourage customer reviews, conduct fake door testing, and analyze marketing campaigns for optimization.

Even after sorting out all of the above, you will still need a general framework that will not only help your team to align with your thought process but will also create standards for continuous improvement. I created this framework after observing many SaaS and software companies.

Marketing a Software as a Service (SaaS) product requires a comprehensive approach that targets each stage of the customer journey.

From creating awareness to generating leads, converting prospects, and engaging customers, employing effective strategies is crucial. In this summary, we will explore key marketing tactics for each stage, including content creation, SEO optimization, compelling landing pages, product demonstrations, testimonials, pricing transparency, call-to-action buttons, onboarding experiences, customer support, and upselling opportunities.

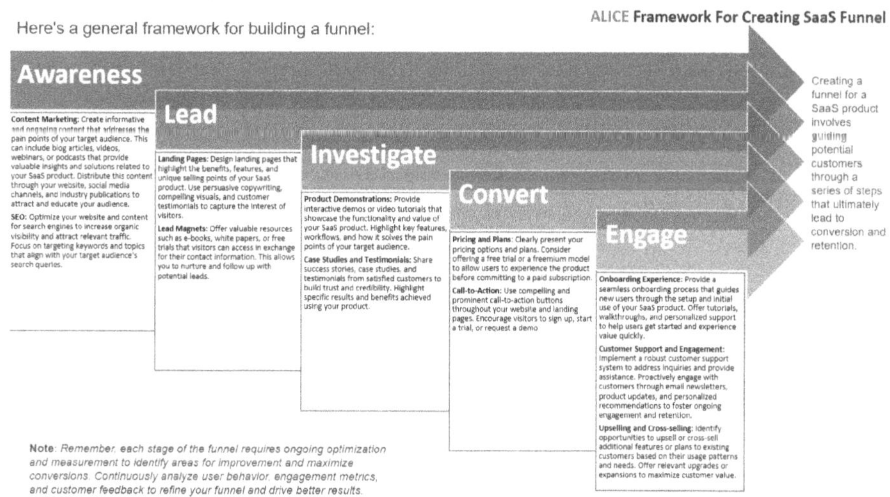

1. **Awareness:** Create valuable content through blog articles, videos, and webinars to address your target audience's pain points. Distribute this content through various channels, including your website, social media, and industry publications. Optimize your website and content for search engines to increase organic visibility.

2. **Lead Generation:** Design compelling landing pages that highlight the benefits and features of your SaaS product to capture visitor interest. Offer valuable resources, such as e-books or free trials, in exchange for contact information to generate leads for further nurturing.

3. **Investigation:** Provide interactive demos or video tutorials to showcase your SaaS product's functionality and address customer pain points. Share success stories and testimonials from satisfied customers to build trust and credibility.

4. **Conversion:** Clearly present pricing options and plans. Consider offering free trials or freemium models to allow users to experience your product before committing. Use compelling and prominent call-to-action buttons to encourage visitors to take the desired action.

5. **Engagement:** Offer a seamless onboarding experience with tutorials and personalized support to help new users get started quickly. Implement a robust customer support system and engage with customers through email newsletters, updates, and personalized recommendations. Identify opportunities for upselling and cross-selling to maximize customer value.

To succeed in marketing a SaaS product, a well-rounded approach encompassing various stages of the customer journey is essential. By creating valuable content, optimizing for search engines, designing compelling landing pages, providing interactive product demonstrations, leveraging testimonials, offering transparent pricing, using effective call-to-action buttons, delivering seamless onboarding experiences, implementing robust customer support, and identifying upselling opportunities, you can effectively attract, engage, and retain customers.

By utilizing these strategies, you can maximize the growth and success of your SaaS business.

Chapter 8

PAID ADVERTISING AND ACQUISITION CHANNELS

Unleashing the Power of Strategic Campaigns

In the dynamic landscape of digital marketing, paid advertising has emerged as a formidable tool for customer acquisition. In this chapter, we will embark on an exhilarating journey through the realm of paid advertising and acquisition channels. We'll delve into the exciting possibilities offered by platforms like Google Ads and social media ads. We'll also uncover the hidden potential of affiliate marketing and strategic partnerships. Get ready to discover innovative strategies that will not only help you attract new customers but also retain them for the long haul.

8.1 Unlocking the Potential of Paid Advertising

The Art of Strategic Campaigns: Selecting a suitable advertising platform

Paid advertising provides a powerful way to reach your target audience and generate leads. Platforms like Google Ads and social media ads offer a range of targeting options and ad formats to engage your potential customers. However, it is essential to craft strategic campaigns that align with your business goals and resonate with your audience. This involves creating compelling ad copy, captivating visuals, and clear calls-to-action that inspire action. By strategically optimizing your campaigns, you can maximize your reach, drive qualified traffic, and increase conversions.

Evaluating and selecting the most suitable advertising platforms can be challenging. It's important to consider factors such as your audience's online behavior, platform reach, cost-effectiveness, and ad format options.

Google Ads, Facebook Ads, and LinkedIn Ads are three popular advertising platforms, each with its own strengths and target audience. Here's a comparison of these platforms and guidance on when to use them:

Google Ads:

- **Audience:** Google Ads has a vast reach and can target users based on their search queries, interests, and website browsing behavior. It is suitable for businesses targeting a wide range of audiences.

- **Ad Formats:** Google Ads offers search ads (text-based ads displayed on search engine results pages), display ads (visual ads shown on websites and apps within the Google Display Network), video ads (played before, during, or after YouTube videos), shopping ads (product listings on Google's Shopping tab), and more.

When to Use: Google Ads is effective for businesses aiming to capture users at the moment they are actively searching for products or services. It is particularly useful for driving website traffic, generating leads, and increasing online sales.

Facebook Ads:

- **Audience:** Facebook Ads allows precise targeting based on demographics, interests, behaviors, and connections. It is suitable for businesses targeting a specific audience segment, such as age groups, interests, or location.

- **Ad Formats:** Facebook Ads offers various ad formats, including image ads, video ads, carousel ads, collection ads, and lead generation ads. It also includes Instagram Ads since Facebook owns Instagram.

When to Use: Facebook Ads is effective for businesses aiming to increase brand awareness, engage with their audience, build a social media following, or drive conversions. It is particularly useful for B2C businesses or those targeting a broad consumer audience.

LinkedIn Ads:

- ✔ **Audience:** LinkedIn Ads focuses on a professional audience and is suitable for B2B businesses or those targeting specific industries, job titles, company sizes, or professional interests.

- ✔ **Ad Formats:** LinkedIn Ads offers sponsored content (native ads in users' LinkedIn feeds), text ads (small ads displayed in the sidebar), and sponsored InMail (personalized messages sent to LinkedIn users' inboxes).

When to Use: LinkedIn Ads is effective for businesses looking to reach professionals, build brand awareness within the business community, recruit talent, promote thought leadership, or generate leads for B2B products or services.

Choosing the right platform depends on your business goals, target audience, and available resources. Consider the following factors:

- **Target** Audience: Identify which platform aligns best with your target audience's demographics, behaviors, and preferences.

- **Ad Format**: Determine which ad formats will effectively convey your message and engage your audience.

- **Budget:** Consider the cost of advertising on each platform and whether it aligns with your budget.

- **Campaign Goals:** Evaluate which platform's features and targeting options are most suitable for your campaign objectives, such as brand awareness, lead generation, or sales.

In many cases, a multi-platform approach can be beneficial to maximize reach and diversify your advertising strategy. Experimenting and monitoring the performance of your campaigns on each platform will help you determine the most effective combination for your specific business needs.

8.2 Harnessing the Power of Targeting:

One of the greatest advantages of paid advertising is the ability to target specific audience segments. Utilize the advanced targeting options provided by advertising platforms to reach the right people based on demographics, interests, behaviors, and online activities. By precisely targeting your ads, you can minimize ad spend wastage and ensure your message reaches those most likely to convert. This strategic approach not only improves the effectiveness of your campaigns but also enhances the overall return on investment.

Finding the right balance between broad and narrow targeting can be challenging. Broad targeting may reach a larger audience but may not be as precise, while narrow targeting may limit reach but potentially yield higher conversions. Regularly monitoring and optimizing your campaigns can help overcome these challenges.

There are several platforms and tools that can be used to implement targeting and optimization in advertising campaigns. Here are a few examples:

- **Google Ads:** Google Ads provides a robust set of targeting options, including demographics, interests, keywords, and remarketing. It is suitable for reaching a wide audience and is particularly effective for search advertising and display advertising.

- **Facebook Ads Manager**: Facebook Ads Manager allows precise targeting based on demographics, interests, behaviors, and connections on Facebook and Instagram. It is effective for reaching a broad consumer audience and offers various ad formats, such as image ads, video ads, and carousel ads.

- **LinkedIn Campaign Manager**: LinkedIn Campaign Manager provides targeting options focused on professionals, including job titles, industries, company size, and more. It is suitable for B2B businesses or those targeting a professional audience.

- **Twitter Ads:** Twitter Ads enables targeting based on interests, demographics, keywords, and followers. It is effective for real-time engagement and reaching a diverse range of audiences.

- **Programmatic Advertising Platforms:** Programmatic advertising platforms, such as Demand-Side Platforms (DSPs), offer automated and data-driven targeting options. These platforms use algorithms and artificial intelligence to optimize ad delivery across multiple ad exchanges and inventory sources.

- **Display Advertising Networks:** Display advertising networks, such as Google Display Network (GDN) and other ad networks, allow you to reach audiences through a network of websites and apps. These networks offer various targeting options and ad formats for visual display ads.

When choosing which platform to use, consider the following factors:

- ✔ **Platform Reach**: Evaluate the reach and user base of each platform. Consider the size and composition of the audience you want to target and select platforms that have a significant presence among your target audience.

- ✔ **Ad Placement Options**: Explore the placement options offered by each platform. Some platforms provide specific ad placements, such as in-feed ads, stories, or search results. Assess whether these placements align with your campaign goals and audience preferences.

- ✔ **Ad Performance Tracking:** Examine the tracking and measurement capabilities of each platform. Look for platforms that offer robust analytics and reporting features, allowing you to monitor campaign performance and make data-driven optimizations.

- ✔ **Ad Targeting Flexibility**: Assess the level of flexibility and granularity in targeting options provided by each platform. Consider whether the platform allows you to target specific demographics, interests, behaviors, or custom audience segments that are relevant to your campaign.

- ✔ **Ad Creative Requirements:** Understand the ad creative requirements and guidelines for each platform. Some platforms may have specific rules regarding ad dimensions, file formats, or content restrictions. Ensure that your creative assets comply with these requirements.

- ✔ **Platform User Behavior**: Research the user behavior and engagement patterns specific to each platform. Understand how users interact with ads and whether the platform's user behavior aligns with your campaign objectives and desired outcomes.

- ✔ **Competitive Landscape:** Consider the competitive landscape on each platform. Evaluate whether your competitors are actively advertising on a particular platform and how saturated the ad space is. This can influence the cost and effectiveness of your campaigns.

- ✔ **Platform Updates and Features:** Stay informed about platform updates and new features that may enhance your targeting and optimization efforts. Platforms frequently introduce new tools, targeting options, or ad formats that can provide additional opportunities to reach and engage your audience.

It's important to note that the best platform or combination of platforms will depend on your specific business, target audience, and advertising objectives. Experimentation, testing, and monitoring the performance of your campaigns across different platforms will help you determine the most effective choices for your advertising efforts.

8.3 Unleashing the Potential of Affiliate Marketing and Partnerships

8.3.1 Building Lucrative Partnerships:

Affiliate marketing and strategic partnerships can significantly amplify your customer acquisition efforts. By collaborating with like-minded businesses or influencers who share your target audience, you can tap into new customer segments and expand your reach. Form mutually beneficial partnerships where you can cross-promote each other's products or services, offer joint campaigns, or create referral programs. This synergy allows you to leverage the existing trust and credibility of your partners, ultimately driving more qualified leads to your business.

8.3.2 Nurturing Affiliate Relationships:

The success of affiliate marketing lies in building strong and long-lasting relationships with your affiliates. Provide them with the necessary resources, promotional materials, and support to effectively promote your offerings. Regular communication, performance incentives, and recognition of their contributions are key to fostering loyalty and motivation among affiliates. By nurturing these relationships, you not only encourage their continued efforts but also foster a sense of partnership and shared success.

8.4 Strategies for Customer Acquisition and Retention

8.4.1 Conversion-Driven Landing Pages:

Paid advertising campaigns should lead to optimized landing pages that drive conversions. Craft landing pages with clear and compelling messaging, attractive designs, and persuasive calls-to-action. Conduct A/B testing to identify the most effective elements and continuously optimize your landing pages for better results. A seamless and engaging user experience on your landing pages increases the chances of converting visitors into paying customers.

Tips and tricks are already discussed above, however one last tip would be to use a good domain or meaningful domain for it by which you audience can easily find you and to keep the form short which can be accessed using any device (responsive design)

8.4.2 Remarketing and Retargeting:

Not every potential customer converts on their first interaction with your brand. Implement remarketing and retargeting strategies to re-engage with users who have shown interest in your offerings but haven't taken the desired action. Display targeted ads across different platforms, reminding them of the value you provide and encouraging them to return. By staying top-of-mind and strategically rekindling their interest, you can improve conversion rates and enhance customer retention.

To select and use various tools for remarketing and retargeting, follow these steps:

- **Define Your Remarketing Goals:** Clarify the specific goals of your remarketing and retargeting campaigns. Are you aiming to drive conversions, increase brand awareness, or improve customer retention? Defining your goals will help you select the right tools and strategies.

- **Choose a Remarketing Platform:** Research and select a remarketing platform that aligns with your goals and target audience. Popular platforms include Google Ads, Facebook Ads, LinkedIn Ads, and specialized retargeting platforms like AdRoll or Criteo.

- **Install Tracking Pixels or Tags:** Set up tracking pixels or tags provided by the remarketing platform on your website or landing pages. These tracking codes allow the platform to identify and track visitors who have interacted with your website or specific pages.

- **Segment Your Audience:** Segment your audience based on their behavior and interactions with your website. Create specific audience lists based on actions such as product page visits, cart abandonment, email sign-ups, or past purchases. This segmentation helps you deliver targeted and personalized ads.

- **Create Compelling Ad Content**: Develop compelling ad content that resonates with your target audience and encourages them to take the desired action. Use persuasive copy, eye-catching visuals, and clear calls-to action (CTAs) to re engage users and remind them of the value your brand offers.

- **Set Up Remarketing Campaigns:** Set up remarketing campaigns on your chosen platform. Define the targeting parameters, budget, ad scheduling, and frequency capping. Customize your campaigns to reach specific audience segments with tailored messaging and ad formats.

- **Monitor and Optimize Performance:** Regularly monitor the performance of your remarketing campaigns. Analyze key metrics such as click-through rates (CTR), conversion rates, cost per conversion, and return on ad spend (ROAS). Use this data to optimize your campaigns by adjusting bids, refining audience targeting, or testing different ad variations.

- **Explore Dynamic Remarketing**: Consider implementing dynamic remarketing, which allows you to display personalized ads to users based on the specific products or pages they viewed on your website. This highly tailored approach can boost engagement and conversion rates.

- **Test and Iterate:**

    - Continuously test different variations of your ads, including messaging, visuals, and CTAs, to identify what resonates best with your audience. A/B testing can help you refine your remarketing campaigns and optimize their performance.

    - Remember to comply with privacy regulations and ensure that you have proper consent or opt-out mechanisms in place for user data collection and remarketing.

By selecting the right remarketing platform, segmenting your audience effectively, creating compelling ad content, and continuously monitoring and optimizing your campaigns, you can leverage remarketing and retargeting to re-engage potential customers, increase conversions, and improve customer retention.

8.4.3 Continuous Tracking and Optimization:

Paid advertising is an ever-evolving landscape, and continuous tracking and optimization are vital for success. Monitor the performance of your campaigns, closely analyze metrics, and make data-driven decisions. Identify areas for improvement, adjust targeting parameters, refine ad copy, and allocate budgets based on performance. By regularly optimizing your campaigns, you can maximize their effectiveness, reduce costs, and drive higher returns on your advertising investment.

Paid advertising and acquisition channels present an exciting and dynamic avenue for customer acquisition. By implementing strategic campaigns, leveraging the power of affiliate marketing and partnerships, and adopting customer acquisition and retention strategies, you can unlock the full potential of paid advertising. Embrace the opportunity to experiment, adapt, and optimize your efforts as you navigate this ever-evolving landscape, ultimately driving sustainable growth and success for your SaaS business.

To continuously track and optimize your advertising campaigns using various tools on different platforms, follow these steps:

- **Set up Conversion Tracking**: Implement conversion tracking on each platform to measure the desired actions taken by users, such as purchases, sign-ups, or form submissions. Use platform-specific tools like Google Ads Conversion Tracking, Facebook Pixel, or LinkedIn Insight Tag.

  Example: Implement Google Ads Conversion Tracking to measure the number of purchases made on your e-commerce website or Facebook Pixel to track sign-ups for your newsletter.

- **Define Key Performance Indicators (KPIs)**: Determine the KPIs that align with your campaign goals, such as conversion rate, click-through rate (CTR), cost per acquisition (CPA), return on ad spend (ROAS), or engagement metrics. These metrics will help you evaluate campaign performance.

  Example: Determine that your primary KPI is the conversion rate, aiming for a target of 5% or a cost per acquisition (CPA) goal of $20.

- **Monitor Campaign Performance**: Regularly monitor your campaigns on each platform and assess their performance against your defined KPIs. Utilize platform-specific reporting dashboards, analytics tools, or third-party analytics solutions like Google Analytics to track key metrics.

  Example: Use the reporting dashboard in Google Ads to monitor impressions, clicks, conversions, and other metrics for your search advertising campaign.

- **Analyze Metrics and Identify Opportunities:** Analyze the campaign data and identify areas for improvement. Look for patterns, trends, or underperforming segments. Determine which platforms, targeting options, or ad creatives are generating the best results and allocate resources accordingly.

  Example: Analyze the campaign data and discover that your display ads are generating a significantly higher CTR compared to search ads, suggesting an opportunity to allocate more budget to display advertising.

- **A/B Testing:** Conduct A/B testing to experiment with different variations of your ads. Test different ad formats, messaging, visuals, targeting parameters, or landing page designs. Measure the performance of each variation to identify the most effective elements.

  Example: Test two variations of your ad copy on Facebook Ads - one with a direct call-to-action and the other highlighting a unique value proposition - to determine which generates a higher conversion rate.

- **Optimize Targeting and Bidding:** Continuously refine your targeting parameters based on performance data. Adjust demographics, interests, placements, or keywords to reach the most relevant audience. Optimize your bidding strategies to maximize ROI and control costs.

  Example: Refine your Google Ads campaign by adjusting keyword bids based on performance data. Increase bids for high-converting keywords and decrease bids for underperforming ones.

- **Refine Ad Copy and Creatives:** Based on data-driven insights, refine your ad copy, visuals, and calls-to-action. Test different headlines, ad formats, ad extensions, or imagery to optimize engagement and click-through rates.

  Example: Modify the headline and imagery of your LinkedIn Ads to align with the preferences and interests of your target audience based on A/B testing results.

- **Budget Allocation:** Analyze the performance of each campaign and allocate your budget strategically. Identify high-performing campaigns and allocate more budget to them while pausing or adjusting underperforming campaigns.

  Example: Analyze the performance of your campaigns on different platforms and decide to allocate more budget to Facebook Ads, where you have consistently achieved a higher ROAS.

- **Regular Performance Reviews**: Conduct regular performance reviews and optimization cycles for your campaigns. Set a cadence for reviewing and adjusting campaign strategies, based on your business needs and the pace of your campaigns.

  Example: Schedule weekly reviews to assess campaign performance and make adjustments. Analyze the click-through rates and conversion rates of your Google Ads campaigns to identify areas for improvement.

- **Stay Updated and Embrace New Features**: Stay updated with platform updates, algorithm changes, and new features. Embrace new targeting options, ad formats, or optimization features offered by the platforms to stay ahead of the competition and leverage the latest tools for better campaign performance.

  Example: Take advantage of the new responsive search ads feature in Google Ads, which automatically adjusts ad combinations to optimize performance and increase relevance.

Remember, optimization is an ongoing process. Continuously track, analyze, and optimize your campaigns on each platform to improve their effectiveness, reduce costs, and drive higher returns on your advertising investment.

Chapter 9

CUSTOMER SUCCESS AND RETENTION

Driving Long-Term Value

In the world of Software-as-a-Service (SaaS) businesses, customer success and retention are critical factors for sustainable growth and profitability. The success of your customers directly impacts the success of your business. In this chapter, we will explore the importance of customer success in the SaaS industry and provide insights on implementing effective customer onboarding and training programs. Additionally, we will discuss how to utilize customer feedback and support to maximize customer retention and create lasting rclationships.

You've successfully acquired a new customer for your SaaS business, but the journey doesn't end there. The biggest mistake many SaaS vendors make is assuming the customer will stay forever. The truth is, that customer retention is just as crucial as acquisition, if not more. In this chapter, we will explore the captivating world of customer success and retention. We'll dive into the strategies and techniques that will help you nurture lifelong partnerships with your customers, ensuring their satisfaction and loyalty.

9.1 Rethinking the Customer Journey:

Acquiring a customer is just the beginning of a beautiful relationship. Embrace the concept of customer success, which focuses on guiding your customers towards achieving their desired outcomes and extracting maximum value from your product or service. By understanding and fulfilling their needs, you can transform satisfied customers into loyal advocates who continue to engage with your business.

To rethink the customer journey and leverage tools or platforms for customer success, follow these steps:

- **Understand Customer Needs and Goals:** Utilize customer feedback, surveys, and data analytics to gain a deep understanding of your customers' needs, pain points, and goals. Identify the key stages of their journey and the challenges they may encounter.

  - ✔ Use tools like surveys and feedback platforms such as SurveyMonkey or Typeform to gather insights into customer needs and goals.

- **Adopt Customer Success Tools:** Implement customer success tools or platforms to streamline your efforts. Examples include customer relationship management (CRM) systems like Salesforce or HubSpot, customer success platforms like Gainsight or Totango, and communication tools like Intercom or Zendesk.

  - ✔ Implement customer relationship management (CRM) systems like Salesforce or HubSpot, which provide robust customer success features and tracking capabilities.

- **Develop a Customer Success Strategy:** Create a customer success strategy that aligns with your customers' goals and helps them achieve success with your product or service. Define key milestones, touchpoints, and metrics to track their progress.

  - ✔ Utilize customer success platforms like Gainsight, Totango, or ClientSuccess to develop and execute your customer success strategy effectively.

- **Personalize Customer Interactions**: Leverage customer success tools to personalize your interactions and communications. Use customer data to provide tailored recommendations, proactive support, and personalized offers or content.

  - ✔ Leverage communication tools like Intercom or Zendesk to deliver personalized messages, targeted recommendations, and support to customers

- **Provide Onboarding Support:** Offer robust onboarding support to guide customers through the initial stages of using your product or service. Utilize onboarding tools or platforms to deliver interactive tutorials, videos, or knowledge base resources.

  - ✔ Use onboarding tools or platforms such as Userpilot or Appcues to guide customers through the onboarding process with interactive tutorials and resources.

- **Implement Customer Health Monitoring:** Utilize customer success platforms to monitor the health and engagement of your customers. Track usage metrics, product adoption, and customer satisfaction scores to identify potential issues and proactively address them.

  - ✔ Utilize customer success platforms like ChurnZero, Natero, or Strikedeck to monitor customer health, track usage metrics, and identify potential issues.

- **Offer Proactive Support and Education:** Utilize customer success tools to provide proactive support and education. Set up automated email campaigns, in-app messaging, or chatbots to offer helpful resources, tips, and best practices to customers.

  - ✔ Use customer support platforms like Freshdesk, Help Scout, or Zendesk to provide proactive support through automated email campaigns, in-app messaging, or chatbots.

- **Collect and Act on Customer Feedback:** Utilize customer feedback tools or platforms to gather insights on customer satisfaction, pain points, and feature requests. Actively listen to customer feedback and use it to drive product improvements and enhance the customer experience.

  - ✔ Leverage feedback tools like Qualtrics, UserVoice, or Delighted to collect and analyze customer feedback, enabling you to make data-driven decisions.

- **Measure and Optimize Customer Success Metrics**: Utilize customer success platforms and analytics tools to measure and optimize customer success metrics. Monitor metrics such as customer retention, churn rate, upsell or cross-sell revenue, and Net Promoter Score (NPS).

  - ✔ Utilize analytics tools such as Mixpanel, Amplitude, or Google Analytics to measure and optimize customer success metrics like retention rate, churn rate, and Net Promoter Score (NPS).

- **Continuously Iterate and Improve**: Regularly review and refine your customer success strategy based on data, customer feedback, and evolving customer needs. Adapt your approach, tools, and processes to ensure ongoing success and value delivery.

  - ✔ Collaborative project management tools like Asana, Trello, or Jira can help you track and manage iterations, ensuring continuous improvement in your customer success efforts.

By rethinking the customer journey and leveraging tools or platforms for customer success, you can foster stronger customer relationships, increase customer satisfaction, and drive long-term engagement and loyalty.

9.1.1 The Impact on Business Success:

Customer success isn't just a feel-good strategy; it directly impacts your business's bottom line. When your customers achieve their goals, they are more likely to renew their subscriptions, upgrade to higher tiers, and recommend your solution to others. By prioritizing customer success, you lay the foundation for sustainable growth, increased customer lifetime value, and a stellar reputation in the market.

To measure the impact of customer success on business success and identify relevant metrics, follow these steps:

- **Customer Retention Rate:** Measure the percentage of customers who continue to use your product or service over a specific period. A higher retention rate indicates successful customer outcomes and a positive impact on business success.

- **Renewal Rate**: Track the percentage of customers who renew their subscriptions or contracts upon expiration. A higher renewal rate demonstrates the effectiveness of your customer success efforts in maintaining long-term customer relationships.

- **Expansion Revenue**: Measure the revenue generated from upselling or cross-selling additional products, services, or upgrades to existing customers. Expansion revenue signifies the success of customer expansion initiatives driven by your customer success strategy.

- **Customer Lifetime Value (CLV):** Calculate the total value a customer generates throughout their entire relationship with your business. A higher CLV indicates successful customer outcomes and the long-term impact on business success.

- **Referral Rate:** Track the number of customer referrals or recommendations made to others. A higher referral rate indicates satisfied customers who advocate for your business, contributing to increased brand awareness and potential new customer acquisition.

- **Net Promoter Score (NPS):** Measure customer loyalty and satisfaction by asking customers to rate the likelihood of recommending your business to others. A higher NPS signifies a positive impact on business success, as satisfied customers are more likely to become promoters.

- **Customer Satisfaction Score (CSAT):** Assess customer satisfaction by gathering feedback on specific interactions or experiences with your product, service, or customer success efforts. A higher CSAT score indicates successful customer outcomes and their impact on business success.

- **Churn Rate:** Track the percentage of customers who cancel or stop using your product or service. A lower churn rate signifies successful customer outcomes and the preservation of recurring revenue, contributing to business success.

- **Customer Engagement Metrics:** Monitor metrics such as usage frequency, feature adoption, and user engagement levels to gauge the effectiveness of your customer success efforts in driving customer value and satisfaction.

- **Revenue Growth:** Assess the overall revenue growth of your business over time, considering factors such as new customer acquisition, customer expansion, and retention. Successful customer outcomes contribute to sustainable revenue growth and overall business success.

By measuring these metrics, you can quantify the impact of your customer success initiatives on business success. It allows you to track customer retention, renewal rates, revenue growth, and customer advocacy, providing insights into the effectiveness of your strategies and the value delivered to customers.

9.2 Unlocking Customer Success through Onboarding and Training

9.2.1 Crafting the Perfect Onboarding Experience:

The onboarding phase sets the tone for the entire customer journey. Design a seamless onboarding experience that empowers customers to quickly understand and utilize your product. Clear instructions, interactive tutorials, and personalized support from dedicated onboarding specialists or customer success managers will ensure customers feel valued and confident from the start.

Challenges in crafting the perfect onboarding experience can include:

- **Complexity:** Addressing the challenge of simplifying complex product features or concepts during the onboarding process.

- **Scalability:** Ensuring the onboarding process can accommodate a growing customer base without sacrificing quality or personalized support.

- **Time Constraints:** Striking a balance between providing thorough onboarding and minimizing the time required for customers to start using the product effectively.

- **Technical Limitations:** Overcoming technical constraints that may hinder the smooth onboarding experience, such as integration issues or system limitations.

User Adoption: Encouraging customers to actively participate in the onboarding process and adopt new behaviors or workflows.

To craft the perfect onboarding experience and overcome potential challenges, follow these steps;

- **Understand Customer Needs:** Gain a deep understanding of your customers' needs, goals, and pain points during the onboarding phase. Conduct customer research, interviews, or surveys to identify common challenges and tailor the onboarding experience accordingly.

- **Define Onboarding Goals:** Clearly define the goals of your onboarding process. Determine what key actions or milestones customers should achieve to consider themselves successfully onboarded. Align these goals with your overall customer success strategy.

- **Develop Onboarding Materials:** Create clear and concise onboarding materials, including instructional videos, step-by-step guides, knowledge base articles, or interactive tutorials. Ensure they are easily accessible and provide relevant information to help customers understand and utilize your product effectively.

- **Personalize the Onboarding Experience:** Customize the onboarding experience based on customer segments, personas, or individual preferences. Utilize customer data to provide personalized onboarding guidance, feature recommendations, or relevant case studies that resonate with their specific needs.

- **Provide Dedicated Support:** Offer dedicated support during the onboarding phase. Assign onboarding specialists or customer success managers to guide customers through the process, address questions, and provide timely assistance. Utilize communication tools or customer success platforms to facilitate seamless interactions.

- **Automate Onboarding Steps:** Streamline the onboarding process by automating repetitive tasks and workflows. Utilize tools like automation platforms (e.g., Zapier or Integromat) or customer onboarding platforms (e.g., Userpilot or Chameleon) to automate user provisioning, email notifications, or user training.

- **Measure Onboarding Success:** Define metrics to measure the success of your onboarding process, such as time to first value, user activation rate, or feature adoption rate. Utilize analytics tools or customer success platforms to track these metrics and identify areas for improvement.

- **Seek Customer Feedback:** Continuously gather feedback from customers about their onboarding experience. Use surveys, interviews, or feedback tools to understand their satisfaction levels, pain points, or suggestions for improvement. Act on this feedback to enhance the onboarding process.

By following these steps and addressing the challenges, you can create a seamless onboarding experience that empowers customers, accelerates their time to value, and sets the stage for a successful and long-lasting customer journey.

9.2.1 Fuelling Success with Tailored Education:

Recognize that each customer is unique and has specific needs. Customize your training and education programs to cater to different customer segments. Whether it's hosting interactive webinars, creating engaging video tutorials, or offering self-paced online courses, provide a variety of resources that empower customers to maximize their product usage. Continuously update and expand these resources to keep pace with evolving customer requirements and new feature developments.

Leading SaaS companies employ various strategies to fuel success with tailored education. Here are some examples of what they do:

- ✔ **Creating a Knowledge Base**: Build a comprehensive knowledge base that serves as a central repository of information, including FAQs, step-by-step guides, and troubleshooting articles. HubSpot's Knowledge Base is an excellent example of this.

- ✔ **Offering Video Tutorials:** Develop a library of video tutorials that demonstrate product features, best practices, and use cases. Slack offers a wide range of video tutorials on their website to help users understand and maximize their platform.

- ✔ **Hosting Interactive Webinars:** Conduct interactive webinars to provide live demonstrations, answer questions, and showcase new features. Companies like Intercom and Salesforce regularly host webinars to engage with their users and provide valuable insights.

- ✔ **Providing Self-Paced Online Courses**: Offer self-paced online courses or certifications to empower customers to deepen their product knowledge. For example, Salesforce Trailhead provides a comprehensive platform for users to learn about their products and earn certifications.

- ✔ **Building a Customer Community:** Establish an online community where customers can connect, share experiences, and learn from each other. Companies like Adobe and Shopify have vibrant community forums where users can ask questions, share tips, and engage with experts.

- **Offering Live Chat or Support:** Provide live chat or support channels to address customer queries in real-time. Intercom, for instance, offers live chat support directly within their platform to assist users promptly.

- **Conducting Virtual Events or Conferences:** Organize virtual events or conferences that bring customers together to learn, network, and explore new features. Salesforce's Dreamforce and HubSpot's INBOUND are notable examples of large-scale virtual events that offer educational sessions and networking opportunities.

- **Sending Targeted Email Campaigns**: Send targeted email campaigns to customers, sharing relevant educational resources, product updates, and tips based on their usage patterns or customer segments. Mailchimp is known for its informative email newsletters that help users optimize their email marketing efforts.

- **Offering Product Walkthroughs:** Provide interactive product walkthroughs or guided tours within the application to familiarize new users with the key features and functionalities. Asana, for example, offers a guided onboarding experience to help users navigate their project management platform.

- **Creating Help Centers or Customer Portals:** Develop comprehensive help centers or customer portals where users can access documentation, training materials, and support resources. Zendesk's Help Center is an example of a well-organized and user-friendly customer portal.

These examples illustrate the diverse approaches SaaS companies take to tailor education and empower their customers. By implementing a combination of these strategies, companies can ensure that customers have access to the resources and support they need to succeed with their products.

9.3 Cultivating Loyalty through Feedback and Support

9.3.1 Proactive Engagement and Support:

Don't wait for customers to reach out with questions or concerns. Take a proactive approach by regularly engaging with them. Conduct check-ins, host informative webinars, and offer workshops to ensure customers are continually reaping the benefits of your solution. By being there every step of the way, you build trust, loyalty, and a reputation for exceptional customer care.

Here are some real-world examples of how companies implement proactive engagement and support strategies:

- ✔ **HubSpot:** HubSpot provides regular check-ins with customers through their Customer Success Managers (CSMs). These CSMs. proactively reach out to customers to assess their needs, offer guidance, and ensure they are maximizing the value of HubSpot's marketing and sales platform.

- ✔ **Adobe:** Adobe hosts informative webinars and workshops for their customers. These sessions cover topics such as new feature releases, best practices, and industry trends. They actively engage with customers to provide educational resources and foster ongoing learning and success.

- ✔ **Zoom:** Zoom offers regular "Zoomtopia" events, which are educational conferences for users and customers. These events feature keynote speeches, interactive sessions, and training workshops to help users make the most of the Zoom platform and stay informed about new updates and features.

- ✔ **Slack:** Slack conducts proactive engagement by hosting Slack Tips & Tricks webinars. These webinars provide insights and best practices on how to use Slack effectively, collaborate efficiently, and optimize communication within teams.

- ✔ **Shopify:** Shopify provides workshops and meetups for their merchants to learn and network with other e-commerce entrepreneurs. These events offer educational sessions, success stories, and practical tips to help merchants grow their online businesses.

- ✔ **Microsoft:** Microsoft offers the "Microsoft Ignite" conference, which is a major event for their customers and users. The conference includes keynote speeches, breakout sessions, and hands-on labs to educate and empower attendees on Microsoft's suite of products and services.

- ✔ **Intercom:** Intercom engages with customers through their "Intercom Insider" program. This program includes regular updates, newsletters, and exclusive content tailored to customers' specific needs and interests, providing ongoing education and insights.

- ✔ **Zendesk:** Zendesk conducts regular webinars and workshops focused on customer service and support best practices. These sessions help users enhance their customer support strategies, utilize Zendesk features effectively, and stay up-to-date with industry trends.

- ✔ **Google:** Google offers the "Google for Startups" program, which provides educational resources, mentorship, and networking opportunities for startup founders. Through workshops, events, and access to Google experts, startups can proactively engage and learn from industry leaders.

- ✔ **Salesforce:** Salesforce conducts the "Trailhead Academy" to provide ongoing training and certification programs for users and administrators of Salesforce products. This proactive approach ensures users stay up-to-date with the latest features and capabilities of the platform.

These examples demonstrate how leading companies take a proactive approach to engage with customers through check-ins, webinars, workshops, conferences, educational programs, and exclusive content. By providing ongoing support and resources, these companies build strong relationships with customers and foster a reputation for exceptional customer care.

9.3.2 Harnessing the Power of Customer Feedback:

Your customers hold invaluable insights that can shape the future of your product. Establish channels for feedback, such as surveys, user forums, or direct communication loops, and actively listen to your customers' suggestions, pain points, and desires. Leverage this feedback to drive continuous improvement, enhance user experience, and develop new features that align with customer needs. By incorporating customer input, you demonstrate that you value their opinions and are committed to their success.

When it comes to gathering customer feedback, businesses have the option to choose between free and paid tools. Free tools such as Google Forms or SurveyMonkey offer basic survey capabilities for collecting feedback, while paid tools like Qualtrics or Medallia provide advanced features, analytics, and customization options to gain more in-depth insights from customer feedback. The choice between free and paid tools depends on the specific needs, budget, and desired level of sophistication for analyzing and acting upon the collected feedback.

9.3.3 Creating a Thriving Customer Community:

Forge a vibrant community where customers can connect, learn, and share their experiences. Cultivate user groups, foster online forums, and organize exclusive events that foster camaraderie among customers. Encourage customers to share success stories, provide testimonials, and refer others to your business. By building a strong customer community, you create a support network that amplifies customer loyalty and propels your brand's reputation.

Forming a customer community on various social media platforms and an internal platform can greatly benefit a SaaS company. Here are some do's and don'ts to consider when establishing and managing a customer community:

Do's:

- ✔ **Foster a Sense of Belonging:** Create a welcoming and inclusive environment where customers feel valued, heard, and connected to each other and your company.

- ✔ **Encourage Engagement and Participation:** Promote active engagement by encouraging customers to share their experiences, ask questions, provide feedback, and offer insights to benefit the community as a whole.

- ✔ **Provide Valuable Content:** Share relevant and informative content, such as product updates, industry news, best practices, and educational resources, to keep the community engaged and help customers derive more value from your SaaS offering.

- ✔ **Facilitate Networking Opportunities:** Encourage networking among community members by providing channels or events where they can connect, collaborate, and learn from one another.

- ✔ **Recognize and Reward Contributions:** Acknowledge and appreciate customers who actively contribute to the community. Highlight their successes, provide badges or incentives, and showcase their expertise to foster a culture of recognition and encouragement.

- ✔ **Listen and Respond:** Actively monitor community discussions and address customer inquiries, concerns, or feedback promptly. Show that you value their input and are committed to their success.

- ✔ **Gather Feedback and Implement Changes:** Leverage the community as a valuable source of feedback. Solicit suggestions, collect insights, and consider implementing improvements based on customer input, reinforcing the notion that their opinions matter.

Don'ts:

- ✖ **Neglect Community Management:** Ensure that the community is well-moderated and managed. Avoid allowing spam, inappropriate content, or disrespectful behavior that can undermine the community's integrity and discourage participation.

- ✖ **Over-Promote or Oversell:** While it's important to share updates and product information, avoid overwhelming the community with excessive promotional content. Maintain a balance between promotional messaging and providing valuable, non-sales-focused discussions.

- **Ignore Negative Feedback:** Embrace constructive criticism and address negative feedback professionally and promptly. Ignoring or dismissing customer concerns can harm your reputation and discourage engagement within the community.

- **Exclude Internal Team Participation:** Encourage internal team members, such as customer support representatives, product managers, or executives, to actively participate in the community. Their presence can provide valuable insights, build trust, and showcase the company's commitment to customer success.

- **Be Inconsistent or Inactive:** Consistency is key to maintaining an engaged community. Regularly provide updates, facilitate discussions, and respond to customer inquiries. Avoid prolonged periods of inactivity, as it may lead to decreased engagement and a sense of abandonment.

- **Violate Privacy or Confidentiality:** Ensure that customer privacy is respected and sensitive information is appropriately handled within the community. Implement clear guidelines and policies to safeguard customer data and maintain confidentiality.

- **Restrict Feedback or Dissenting Opinions:** Embrace diverse perspectives and encourage open discussions within the community. Avoid suppressing or censoring feedback or dissenting opinions, as they can provide valuable insights and foster a culture of transparency.

By following these insights, a SaaS company can effectively form and nurture a customer community on various social media platforms and an internal platform. This community can foster stronger relationships, drive engagement, and contribute to the overall success of the company and its customers.

Here are some real-life examples of SaaS companies that have successfully built customer communities and the names of their communities:

- **Salesforce:** Salesforce has a thriving customer community known as the "Trailblazer Community." It is a platform where users, developers, administrators, and partners can connect, share knowledge, collaborate, and learn from each other.

- **HubSpot:** HubSpot has a community called the "HubSpot Community." It serves as a space for HubSpot users, marketers, and sales professionals to come together, ask questions, exchange ideas, and get insights from industry experts.

- **Shopify:** Shopify has a community forum named the "Shopify Community." It is a gathering place for Shopify merchants to connect, share experiences, ask questions, and learn from each other about running successful online businesses.

- **Slack:** Slack's community is called the "Slack Community." It is an online community where users and developers come together to discuss tips, tricks, and best practices for using Slack effectively in their teams and organizations.

- **Adobe:** Adobe has a customer community called the "Adobe Community." It is a platform where Adobe product users, designers, and developers engage with one another, share knowledge, and provide support for Adobe products and services.

- **Atlassian:** Atlassian has a community platform called "Atlassian Community." It is a space for users of Atlassian products like Jira, Confluence, and Trello to connect, share best practices, ask questions, and get support from other users and Atlassian experts.

- **Zendesk:** Zendesk has a community known as the "Zendesk Community." It is a place where users of Zendesk products can collaborate, share insights, get tips, and learn about best practices for customer service and support.

- **Intercom**: Intercom has a community called the "Intercom Community." It serves as a platform for Intercom users, marketers, and customer support professionals to come together, share knowledge, and discuss strategies for improving customer engagement and support.

These examples demonstrate how SaaS companies create dedicated customer communities to facilitate knowledge-sharing, networking, and collaboration among their users. These communities provide valuable resources, foster engagement, and contribute to the overall success of the company and its customers.

Customer success and retention are crucial for the long-term viability of SaaS businesses. By prioritizing customer success, implementing effective onboarding and training programs, and leveraging customer feedback and support, companies can drive value, increase customer satisfaction, and build lasting relationships. Remember, customer success is an ongoing journey that requires continuous improvement and a deep understanding of your customers' evolving needs. By investing in customer success, you are investing in the growth and success of your own.

Notes

Chapter 10

MEASURING SAAS SUCCESS

Metrics and Tools for Effective Evaluation

In the dynamic world of Software-as-a-Service (SaaS) businesses, measuring success is crucial for making informed decisions and driving growth. This chapter delves into the realm of metrics and tools that enable effective evaluation of your SaaS business. By identifying key performance indicators (KPIs), exploring analytics tools, and embracing data-driven decision-making, you will gain valuable insights to optimize your marketing campaigns, enhance customer experiences, and ultimately achieve long-term success.

10.1 Identifying Key Performance Indicators (KPIs) for SaaS Success

10.1.1 Defining Your SaaS Success Objectives:

To effectively measure success, you must establish clear objectives that align with your SaaS business's overarching goals. These objectives could include metrics such as customer acquisition, revenue growth, churn rate, customer lifetime value (CLTV), or user engagement. By defining your KPIs, you create a framework for evaluating performance and tracking progress toward your desired outcomes.

10.1.2 Key Metrics for SaaS Success:

1. Monthly Recurring Revenue (MRR) and Annual Run Rate (ARR) are key metrics used in the SaaS industry to measure the financial performance and growth of a subscription-based business.

   a. **Monthly Recurring Revenue (MRR):**

   Monthly Recurring Revenue (MRR) refers to the predictable and recurring revenue generated from subscription-based customers over a month. It represents the revenue that a company can expect to receive on a monthly basis.

   To calculate MRR, sum up the monthly subscription fees of all active customers. Exclude any one-time fees or variable charges. For example, if you have 100 customers with monthly subscription fees of $50, $100, and $150, respectively, your MRR would be $50 + $100 + $150 = $300.

   MRR is a valuable metric for understanding the revenue stream and growth potential of a SaaS business on a month-to-month basis.

   b. **Annual Run Rate (ARR):**

   Annual Run Rate (ARR) estimates the projected annual revenue of a company based on its current MRR. It assumes that the revenue generated in the current month will continue for the entire year.

   To calculate ARR, multiply the MRR by 12. For example, if your MRR is $300, your ARR would be $300 x 12 = $3,600.

   ARR provides a useful snapshot of the company's revenue potential for the entire year and is commonly used to measure and forecast growth.

   Both MRR and ARR are critical metrics that SaaS businesses use to track and evaluate their revenue performance, assess growth trends, and make informed business decisions. These metrics are particularly valuable when considering factors such as customer churn, expansion revenue, and overall business scalability.

2. **Customer Acquisition Cost (CAC) and Customer Lifetime Value (CLTV)** are important metrics used in the SaaS industry to evaluate the financial aspects of acquiring and retaining customers.

    a. **Customer Acquisition Cost (CAC):** Customer Acquisition Cost (CAC) is the average cost a company incurs to acquire a new customer. It includes all the expenses related to sales and marketing efforts, such as advertising, marketing campaigns, sales team salaries, and other associated costs, divided by the number of new customers acquired within a specific period.

    To calculate CAC, add up all the costs associated with customer acquisition during a given period and divide it by the number of new customers acquired. For example, if you spent $10,000 on marketing and sales efforts to acquire 100 new customers, your CAC would be $10,000 ÷ 100 = $100.

    Measuring CAC helps companies understand the efficiency of their customer acquisition strategies and assess the return on investment for acquiring new customers.

    b. **Customer Lifetime Value (CLTV):** Customer Lifetime Value (CLTV) is the predicted total revenue a company expects to generate from a single customer throughout their entire relationship with the business. CLTV takes into account the recurring revenue from subscriptions, additional purchases, and any other revenue streams associated with the customer.

    To calculate CLTV, multiply the average revenue generated from a customer per period (such as monthly or annually) by the average customer lifespan or retention period. For example, if the average customer spends $50 per month and stays with the company for two years, the CLTV would be $50 x 12 months x 2 years = $1,200.

CLTV helps businesses understand the long-term value of acquiring and retaining customers, guiding decisions regarding customer acquisition strategies, pricing, and customer retention efforts.

By analyzing CAC in Google Ads (to calculate CAC based on advertising costs) and CLTV (manually using excel) together, businesses can assess the cost-effectiveness of their customer acquisition efforts and evaluate the profitability of acquiring and retaining customers. It allows companies to make data-driven decisions and optimize their strategies to maximize revenue and growth.

2. Churn rate and retention metrics are essential measurements that assess customer retention and loyalty in the SaaS industry.

    a. **Churn Rate:** Churn rate refers to the rate at which customers cancel or unsubscribe from a SaaS product or service over a specific period. It is a critical metric for understanding customer attrition and the effectiveness of customer retention strategies.

    To calculate churn rate, divide the number of customers lost during a specific period by the total number of customers at the beginning of that period. Multiply the result by 100 to express it as a percentage. For example, if you started the month with 100 customers and lost 5 customers during that month, your churn rate would be (5/100) x 100 = 5%.

    Monitoring churn rate helps businesses assess customer satisfaction, identify potential issues, and take proactive measures to improve customer retention.

b. **Retention Metrics:** Retention metrics provide insights into how well a SaaS company is retaining customers and building long-term relationships. Some commonly used retention metrics include:

   i. **Customer Retention Rate:** This metric measures the percentage of customers that continue using the product or service over a specific period. It is calculated by subtracting the churn rate from 100%. For example, if the churn rate is 5%, the retention rate would be 100% - 5% = 95%.

   ii. **Average Revenue per User (ARPU):** ARPU measures the average revenue generated by each customer over a specific period. It helps evaluate the overall value derived from the customer base.

   iii. **Cohort Analysis:** Cohort analysis tracks the behavior and performance of customers grouped based on their subscription or acquisition date. It helps identify trends and patterns that can inform strategies to improve customer retention and engagement.

Monitoring retention and churn metrics using any CRM system allows businesses to identify opportunities for improving customer experiences, increasing satisfaction, and implementing strategies to reduce churn. By focusing on retention, companies can build a loyal customer base and drive long-term growth.

3. Net Promoter Score (NPS) and customer satisfaction metrics are used to assess customer sentiment and gauge the overall satisfaction and loyalty of customers in the SaaS industry.

   a. **Net Promoter Score (NPS)**: Net Promoter Score (NPS) measures the likelihood of customers to recommend a company's product or service to others. It is based on a single question: "On a scale of 0 to 10, how likely are you to recommend our product/service to a friend or colleague?" Respondents are then categorized into three groups:

i. **Promoters (score 9-10):** Customers who are highly satisfied and likely to promote the product/service.

ii. **Passives (score 7-8):** Customers who are somewhat satisfied but not enthusiastic promoters.

iii. **Detractors (score 0-6):** Customers who are dissatisfied and may even spread negative word-of-mouth.

To calculate NPS, subtract the percentage of detractors from the percentage of promoters. The result can range from -100 to +100, representing the overall sentiment of customers.

NPS provides an indication of customer loyalty and helps identify areas for improvement to enhance customer satisfaction and advocacy.

4. **Customer Satisfaction Metrics:** Customer satisfaction metrics assess how satisfied customers are with a company's product or service. Some common metrics used include:

   a. **Customer Satisfaction Score (CSAT):** CSAT measures the satisfaction level of customers based on specific interactions or experiences. It is typically measured through a survey asking customers to rate their satisfaction on a scale, such as from 1 to 5 or 1 to 10.

   b. **Customer Effort Score (CES):** CES evaluates the ease of doing business with a company. It measures the level of effort customers have to exert to accomplish a task, such as resolving an issue or using a product feature.

   c. **Customer Happiness Index (CHI):** CHI combines various metrics, including satisfaction, loyalty, and advocacy, to provide an overall measure of customer happiness.

These customer satisfaction metrics help businesses understand the strengths and weaknesses of their offerings, identify areas for improvement, and drive customer-centric strategies.

By regularly measuring NPS and customer satisfaction metrics, businesses can track customer sentiment, identify opportunities for improvement, and take action to enhance customer experiences and loyalty. This, in turn, can lead to increased customer retention and positive word-of-mouth referrals.

10.2 Exploring Metrics and Analytics Tools for Data-Driven Decision-Making

10.2.1 Leveraging Analytics Tools:

Analytics and reporting tools play a crucial role in the success of a SaaS business by providing valuable insights into customer behavior, product usage, and sales performance. In this chapter, we will explore some commonly used analytics and reporting tools that can help SaaS companies track and analyze key metrics.

a. **Google Analytics and Other Website Analytics Platforms:** Google Analytics is a widely used web analytics platform that provides in-depth insights into website traffic, user behavior, and conversion rates. It allows businesses to track various metrics, such as page views, session duration, bounce rates, and conversion goals. With Google Analytics, SaaS companies can gain a comprehensive understanding of how users interact with their websites and identify opportunities for optimization.

   In addition to Google Analytics, there are other website analytics platforms available, such as Adobe Analytics and Matomo (formerly Piwik). These tools offer similar features and provide detailed analytics to monitor website performance and user engagement.

b. **SaaS-Specific Analytics Tools**: SaaS-specific analytics tools are designed to track and analyze metrics specific to SaaS products. These tools offer insights into product usage, user engagement, and customer behavior. Two popular examples of such tools are Mixpanel and Amplitude.

- Mixpanel enables SaaS companies to track user actions within their products, such as feature usage, onboarding progress, and conversion funnels. It provides detailed analytics to help businesses understand how users engage with their product and make data-driven decisions for improving user experiences.
- Amplitude is another powerful analytics tool for SaaS businesses. It allows companies to track user behavior, retention rates, and product usage patterns. With Amplitude, SaaS companies can gain actionable insights into user engagement, retention strategies, and product optimization.

c. **Customer Relationship Management (CRM) Systems**: CRM systems are essential for managing sales activities and customer data. These tools help SaaS companies track and organize customer interactions, manage leads and opportunities, and monitor the sales pipeline. Some popular CRM systems include Salesforce, HubSpot CRM, and Zoho CRM.

   CRM systems provide SaaS businesses with a centralized platform to store customer information, track customer interactions, and analyze sales performance. They enable effective lead management, sales forecasting, and customer segmentation, helping businesses make informed decisions to improve sales effectiveness and customer satisfaction.

So, in conclusion, any specified analytics and reporting tools are indispensable for SaaS companies seeking to gain insights into their website performance, product usage, customer behavior, and sales activities. Tools like Google Analytics provide website-specific metrics, while SaaS-specific analytics tools like Mixpanel and Amplitude offer in-depth insights into product usage and engagement.

Furthermore, CRM systems serve as valuable platforms for managing customer relationships and sales processes. By leveraging these tools, SaaS businesses can make data-driven decisions, optimize their products, improve customer experiences, and drive growth.

In addition to Google Analytics, there are other website analytics platforms available, such as Adobe Analytics and Matomo (formerly Piwik). These tools offer similar features and provide detailed analytics to monitor website performance and user engagement.

It is important for SaaS companies to carefully select the right analytics and reporting tools that align with their specific needs and objectives. Regular analysis and reporting using these tools enable businesses to track key performance indicators, identify areas for improvement, and make informed strategic decisions to propel their success in the competitive SaaS industry.

6. **Customer Success and Support Tools**

Customer success and support are vital aspects of running a successful SaaS business. In this chapter, we will explore various tools that can help SaaS companies effectively manage customer support, drive customer success, and gather valuable feedback.

1. **Customer Support Ticketing Systems:** Customer support ticketing systems are essential tools for managing customer inquiries, issues, and requests. They provide a centralized platform for tracking and resolving customer tickets efficiently. Two popular examples of customer support ticketing systems are Zendesk and Freshdesk.

    a. **Zendesk** offers a comprehensive suite of customer support tools, including ticket management, live chat, and knowledge base management. It enables businesses to provide timely and personalized support, track customer interactions, and measure support team performance.

b. **Freshdesk** is another robust ticketing system that streamlines customer support processes. It offers features such as ticket management, automation, and self-service options to enhance customer satisfaction and improve support team efficiency.

2. **Customer Success Management Platforms**: Customer success management platforms are designed to help SaaS companies proactively manage and nurture customer relationships, driving customer success and retention. These platforms provide insights into customer health, usage patterns, and engagement. Two prominent examples are Gainsight and Totango.

   a. **Gainsight** offers a wide range of features, including customer health scoring, product adoption tracking, and automated workflows for proactive customer engagement. It enables SaaS businesses to identify at-risk customers, provide personalized onboarding, and drive customer satisfaction and loyalty.

   b. **Totango** is a customer success platform that helps SaaS companies monitor customer behavior, measure product usage, and track customer health. It provides analytics and automation capabilities to identify upsell and cross-sell opportunities, reduce churn, and deliver personalized customer experiences.

6. **Feedback and Survey Tools**: Feedback and survey tools allow SaaS companies to gather valuable insights from customers, enabling them to understand customer satisfaction, gather product feedback, and identify areas for improvement. Examples of feedback and survey tools include SurveyMonkey and Typeform.

   o **SurveyMonkey is** a popular online survey tool that helps businesses create and distribute surveys to collect feedback from customers. It offers a range of survey templates and analytics capabilities to analyze and interpret survey responses.

- **Typeform is** another versatile survey tool that enables SaaS companies to create interactive and engaging surveys. It offers features like conditional logic and personalized question paths to provide a user-friendly survey experience.

Using these feedback and survey tools, SaaS companies can gain a deeper understanding of customer needs, gather actionable feedback, and continuously improve their products and services.

In conclusion, customer success and support tools are essential for SaaS companies to deliver exceptional customer experiences, drive customer satisfaction, and ensure long-term success. Customer support ticketing systems like Zendesk and Freshdesk streamline support processes, while customer success management platforms such as Gainsight and Totango help proactively manage customer relationships.

Additionally, feedback and survey tools like SurveyMonkey and Typeform enable SaaS businesses to gather valuable insights from customers, helping them make data-driven decisions and improve their products and services.

Choosing the right customer success and support tools that align with specific business needs is crucial. By leveraging these tools effectively, SaaS companies can enhance customer satisfaction, reduce churn, and build strong, long-lasting customer relationships in the competitive SaaS industry.

7. Marketing Automation and Campaign Analytics

Marketing automation and campaign analytics are essential components of a successful marketing strategy for SaaS companies. In this chapter, we will explore key tools that enable effective marketing automation and provide detailed analytics for campaign tracking.

1. **Marketing Automation Platforms:** Marketing automation platforms streamline and automate marketing processes, allowing SaaS companies to execute targeted campaigns and track their performance. Two popular examples of marketing automation platforms are HubSpot and Marketo.

a. **HubSpot** offers a comprehensive suite of marketing automation tools, including email marketing, lead nurturing, lead scoring, and customer relationship management (CRM) integration. It allows businesses to automate marketing campaigns, track customer interactions, and measure the effectiveness of marketing efforts.

b. **Marketo** is another powerful marketing automation platform that enables SaaS companies to create personalized and targeted campaigns. It provides features such as lead management, email marketing, and campaign analytics to drive customer engagement and conversions.

These marketing automation platforms help SaaS companies optimize marketing workflows, nurture leads, and measure the success of their campaigns.

8. **Email Marketing Software with Detailed Analytics**

Marketing automation and campaign analytics tools are essential for SaaS companies to streamline marketing processes, track campaign performance, and optimize marketing efforts

- ✔ **Email marketing** remains a powerful tool for SaaS companies to engage with customers and drive conversions. Email marketing software with detailed analytics provides insights into email performance, audience engagement, and conversion rates. Examples of such tools include Mailchimp and Campaign Monitor.

    - **Mailchimp** offers robust email marketing features along with advanced analytics. It provides detailed reports on open rates, click-through rates, and audience segmentation. These insights help businesses optimize their email campaigns and deliver relevant content to subscribers.

    - **Campaign Monitor** is another popular email marketing software that offers advanced analytics to track email performance. It provides metrics like delivery rates, engagement rates, and conversion tracking.

These analytics help SaaS companies measure the effectiveness of their email campaigns and make data-driven improvements.

- ✔ **Social Media Analytics Tools:** Social media plays a significant role in the marketing efforts of SaaS companies. Social media analytics tools provide insights into audience engagement, reach, and conversion rates. Examples of social media analytics tools include Sprout Social and Hootsuite.

    - **Sprout Social** offers a comprehensive social media management platform with robust analytics capabilities. It provides data on audience demographics, engagement metrics, and content performance across various social media platforms. These insights enable businesses to measure the impact of their social media campaigns and optimize their strategies.

    - **Hootsuite** is another popular social media management tool that offers detailed analytics for tracking social media performance. It provides metrics like follower growth, engagement rates, and click-through rates. These analytics help SaaS companies assess the effectiveness of their social media efforts and identify areas for improvement.

By utilizing marketing automation platforms, email marketing software with detailed analytics, and social media analytics tools, SaaS companies can automate marketing workflows, track campaign performance, and make data-driven decisions to optimize their marketing strategies.

In conclusion, marketing automation platforms like HubSpot and Marketo enable businesses to automate and measure the effectiveness of their marketing campaigns. Email marketing software with detailed analytics, such as Mailchimp and Campaign Monitor, provide insights into email performance and audience engagement. Social media analytics tools like Sprout Social and Hootsuite offer valuable metrics to track social media campaign effectiveness.

By leveraging these tools effectively, SaaS companies can improve campaign targeting, enhance customer engagement, and drive better marketing outcomes. It is crucial to select the right tools that align with specific marketing goals and objectives, and regularly analyze campaign analytics to make informed decisions and optimize marketing strategies in the dynamic SaaS industry.

10.2.2 A/B Testing for Optimization:

A/B testing, also known as split testing, is a powerful technique that enables you to compare different versions of your marketing campaigns, website layouts, or product features to determine which yields better results. Through this iterative process of testing variations and analyzing the results, you can make data-driven decisions to optimize conversions, enhance user experiences, and improve overall performance.

There are several tools and products available that can facilitate A/B testing in the context of SaaS marketing. Here are a few examples:

- ✔ **Optimizely:** Optimizely is a popular A/B testing and experimentation platform that allows you to create and run A/B tests without requiring extensive technical knowledge. It provides a user-friendly interface for designing variations, targeting specific audience segments, and analyzing test results.

- ✔ **Google Optimize:** Google Optimize is a free A/B testing and personalization platform offered by Google. It integrates seamlessly with Google Analytics, allowing you to create experiments and track key metrics directly within the Google Analytics interface. Google Optimize offers both visual and code-based editing options for creating variations.

- ✔ **VWO (Visual Website Optimizer):** VWO is a comprehensive A/B testing and conversion optimization platform. It offers a range of features, including A/B testing, multivariate testing, heatmaps, and user behavior analysis. VWO provides an intuitive interface for creating and managing experiments and provides in-depth analytics to evaluate test performance.

- ✔ **Convert:** Convert is a flexible A/B testing and personalization platform that caters to both marketers and developers. It offers advanced targeting options, customizable experiment setups, and real-time analytics. Convert also integrates with various third-party tools and platforms, allowing for seamless data integration.

These tools provide the necessary infrastructure and capabilities to conduct A/B tests efficiently, track performance metrics, and generate insights for optimizing your SaaS marketing campaigns. By utilizing these tools, you can streamline the A/B testing process and leverage data to make informed decisions that drive better outcomes for your business.

10.3 Conducting A/B Testing and Optimizing Marketing Campaigns

10.3.1 Optimizing Marketing Campaigns:

Effective marketing campaigns drive customer acquisition and engagement. By continuously monitoring and optimizing your campaigns, you can refine your messaging, targeting, and channels to maximize results. Track key metrics, such as click-through rates, conversion rates, and customer acquisition costs, to identify areas for improvement and allocate resources effectively.

To optimize your marketing campaigns without incurring additional costs, you can leverage various free tools that provide valuable insights and analytics. Here are some examples:

- **Google Analytics:** Google Analytics is a powerful and widely-used web analytics tool that allows you to track and analyze website traffic, user behavior, and conversion rates. It provides valuable insights into the performance of your marketing campaigns, allowing you to measure the effectiveness of different channels, landing pages, and campaigns. With Google Analytics, you can monitor metrics like click-through rates, bounce rates, and conversion rates to identify areas for optimization.

- **Facebook Ads Manager**: If you are running Facebook advertising campaigns, Facebook Ads Manager provides a built-in analytics tool for tracking and optimizing your campaigns. It allows you to monitor key metrics like reach, engagement, and conversions. With Facebook Ads Manager, you can analyze the performance of your ads, test different ad variations, and make data-driven decisions to improve campaign effectiveness.

- **Mailchimp**: Mailchimp is a popular email marketing platform that offers a free plan with basic analytics features. It provides insights into the performance of your email campaigns, including open rates, click-through rates, and subscriber engagement. With Mailchimp, you can track the effectiveness of your email marketing efforts and make improvements based on the data you gather.

- **Bitly:** Bitly is a URL shortening service that also offers basic link analytics. By shortening your campaign URLs with Bitly, you can track click-through rates, geographic data, and referral sources. This allows you to monitor the performance of your links across different channels and optimize your campaigns accordingly.

- **Google Search Console**: Google Search Console is a free tool provided by Google that helps you monitor and optimize the visibility of your website in Google search results. It provides data on organic search traffic, click-through rates, and keyword performance. By analyzing this data, you can identify opportunities to improve your website's visibility and optimize your content strategy.

By utilizing these free tools effectively, you can gather valuable data, track key metrics, and make informed decisions to optimize your marketing campaigns. Remember to choose the tools that best align with your specific needs and objectives to drive the success of your SaaS marketing efforts without incurring additional costs.

10.3.2 Data-Driven Decision-Making:

Embrace a culture of data-driven decision-making within your SaaS business. Collect and analyze data from various sources, including user behavior, customer feedback, and market trends. This enables you to make informed decisions, identify growth opportunities, and align your strategies with the evolving needs of your target audience.

To facilitate data-driven decision-making, there are several tools available that can help you collect, analyze, and interpret data effectively. Here are some examples:

- **Google Analytics:** Google Analytics is a powerful tool that provides comprehensive data on website traffic, user behavior, and conversion rates. By leveraging Google Analytics, you can gain insights into the performance of your website, track user interactions, and understand how visitors engage with your content. This data can inform your decision-making process and help you optimize your website and marketing strategies.

- **Hotjar:** Hotjar is a user behavior analytics and feedback tool that offers heatmaps, session recordings, and surveys. Heatmaps visualize user interactions and show where visitors are clicking and scrolling on your website. Session recordings provide video recordings of user sessions, allowing you to see how users navigate your site. Surveys help collect direct feedback from users. By using Hotjar, you can gain a deeper understanding of user behavior, identify areas for improvement, and make data-driven decisions to enhance user experiences.

- **SurveyMonkey:** SurveyMonkey is an online survey tool that allows you to create and distribute surveys to gather customer feedback. With SurveyMonkey, you can design customized surveys and collect responses to gain insights into customer preferences, satisfaction levels, and pain points. By analyzing the survey data, you can uncover valuable information that can guide your decision-making and help you tailor your products and services to better meet customer needs.

- **SEMrush:** SEMrush is an all-in-one digital marketing toolkit that provides competitive analysis, keyword research, and SEO analytics. It allows you to analyze your competitors' online presence, identify popular keywords in your industry, and track your website's search engine rankings. By leveraging SEMrush, you can gain valuable insights into market trends, optimize your content strategy, and align your SEO efforts with the demands of your target audience.

- **Social media analytics tools:** Social media platforms often offer built-in analytics tools that provide insights into audience demographics, engagement rates, and content performance. Platforms like Facebook, Twitter, and LinkedIn offer analytics dashboards where you can track key metrics such as post reach, engagement, and click-through rates. By monitoring these metrics, you can understand how your social media content is resonating with your audience and adjust your strategies accordingly.

By utilizing these data-driven decision-making tools effectively, you can collect and analyze data from multiple sources, gain insights into user behavior and preferences, and align your strategies with the evolving needs of your target audience. Remember to select the tools that best fit your business objectives and leverage the data to make informed decisions that drive the growth and success of your SaaS business.

CHAPTER 11

SCALING AND GROWTH STRATEGIES

In the fast-paced world of Software-as-a-Service (SaaS) businesses, scaling and growth are essential for long-term success. This chapter explores effective strategies to scale your SaaS marketing efforts, expand into new markets and verticals, and navigate the challenges and opportunities that come with growth. By implementing these strategies, you can propel your SaaS business to new heights and unlock its full potential.

11.1 Strategies for Scaling SaaS Marketing Efforts

11.1.1 Data-Driven Marketing:

Leverage the power of data to optimize and scale your marketing efforts. Analyze user behavior, engagement metrics, and conversion rates to identify successful marketing channels and campaigns. By focusing your resources on the most effective channels, you can maximize your reach, increase customer acquisition, and drive sustainable growth by utilizing tools like Google Analytics and customer relationship management (CRM) software.

Example: With Google Analytics, you can track user behavior, engagement metrics, and conversion rates on your website. By integrating this data with your CRM system, such as Salesforce or HubSpot, you can gain deeper insights into your customers' journey and behavior. By analyzing this data, you can identify successful marketing channels and campaigns, optimize your marketing efforts, and allocate resources to maximize reach, increase customer acquisition, and drive sustainable growth.

11.2 Marketing Automation:

Implement marketing automation tools to streamline and scale your marketing processes. Automation allows you to nurture leads, send personalized campaigns, and automate repetitive tasks, freeing up your team's time to focus on strategic initiatives. By automating your marketing efforts, you can efficiently scale your campaigns while maintaining a personalized customer experience. Implement marketing automation tools such as **Marketo or Mailchimp** in conjunction with your CRM system.

When it comes to marketing automation, businesses have a variety of free and paid tools to choose from. Some popular free marketing automation tools include MailChimp, Hootsuite, and MailerLite, offering features like email marketing, social media scheduling, and basic customer segmentation. On the other hand, paid marketing automation tools such as HubSpot, Marketo, and Pardot provide advanced functionalities like lead scoring, personalized workflows, and CRM integration, allowing for more sophisticated automation and customization options. The key features that differentiate these paid tools include robust analytics and reporting, advanced lead nurturing capabilities, and seamless integration with other marketing and sales platforms.

Here's a list of marketing automation tools, along with their key features and when to use each tool:

- **MailChimp (Free):**
    - **Key Feature:** Easy-to-use email marketing platform with customizable templates, audience segmentation, and basic automation features.
    - **When to Use:** Ideal for small businesses or startups looking for a user-friendly tool to manage email marketing campaigns and basic automation workflows.

- **Hootsuite (Free):**
    - **Key Feature:** Social media management platform that allows scheduling, monitoring, and analyzing social media content across multiple channels.
    - **When to Use:** Useful for businesses focusing on social media marketing and wanting to streamline content scheduling and engagement.

- **MailerLite (Free):**
    - **Key Feature:** All-in-one email marketing tool offering drag-and-drop email builder, automation workflows, landing page creation, and subscriber management.
    - **When to Use:** Suitable for small to medium-sized businesses that need a comprehensive email marketing solution with basic automation capabilities.

- **HubSpot (Paid):**
    - **Key Feature:** Robust marketing automation platform with advanced lead nurturing, behavior-based automation, CRM integration, and detailed analytics.
    - **When to Use:** Recommended for businesses of any size looking for a powerful all-in-one marketing automation tool with advanced features and scalable capabilities.

- **Marketo (Paid):**
    - **Key Feature:** Enterprise-level marketing automation platform offering lead management, email marketing, A/B testing, advanced analytics, and CRM integration.
    - **When to Use:** Ideal for larger businesses or enterprises that require a sophisticated marketing automation solution with extensive scalability and customization options.

- **Pardot (Paid):**
    - **Key Feature:** B2B-focused marketing automation tool offering lead generation, nurturing, and scoring, email marketing, ROI reporting, and seamless Salesforce integration.
    - **When to Use:** Suitable for B2B companies, particularly those leveraging Salesforce CRM, seeking comprehensive marketing automation capabilities tailored for their sales funnel.

- **Active Campaign (Paid):**
    - **Key Feature:** Customer experience automation platform with email marketing, lead scoring, website tracking, CRM integration, and powerful automation workflows.
    - **When to Use:** Recommended for businesses looking for an all-in-one marketing automation tool that emphasizes personalized customer journeys and automation flexibility.

- **ConvertKit (Paid):**
    - **Key Feature:** Email marketing platform designed for content creators and bloggers, offering subscriber management, automation rules, landing page creation, and customizable forms.
    - **When to Use:** Ideal for individuals or small businesses in the content creation space, such as bloggers, podcasters, or online course creators, seeking a simple yet effective email marketing solution.

Each tool offers unique features and caters to different business needs. The choice of the right marketing automation tool depends on factors such as budget, business size, specific requirements, and desired level of automation sophistication.

By integrating these tools, you can streamline and scale your marketing processes. Marketing automation allows you to nurture leads, send personalized campaigns, and automate repetitive tasks. For example, you can set up automated email campaigns triggered by specific actions or behaviors of your leads or customers. By leveraging marketing automation, you can efficiently scale your campaigns, maintain a personalized customer experience, and free up your team's time to focus on strategic initiatives

11.3 Performance Marketing:

Embrace performance marketing strategies such as pay-per-click (PPC) advertising, affiliate marketing, and influencer partnerships. These strategies enable you to scale your marketing efforts based on measurable results and a clear return on investment (ROI). By aligning your marketing spend with tangible outcomes, you can effectively allocate resources and drive scalable growth.

When evaluating the performance of a performance marketing campaign, it is important to consider several key metrics that provide insights into its effectiveness. While the importance of metrics may vary depending on campaign objectives and business goals, here are some insights to consider:

- **Conversion Rate:** The conversion rate is a crucial metric that indicates the success of a campaign in driving desired actions. It is essential to track the conversion rate specific to the campaign's objectives, whether it's generating sales, form submissions, or sign-ups.

- **Return on Ad Spend (ROAS):** ROAS is a vital metric as it measures the revenue generated in relation to the advertising investment. A higher ROAS signifies better profitability and efficiency, indicating that the campaign is delivering strong returns.

- **Cost per Acquisition (CPA):** CPA helps determine the average cost incurred to acquire a new customer or lead. It is important to compare the CPA against the lifetime value (LTV) of customers to ensure the campaign's profitability and long-term success.

- **Click-Through Rate (CTR):** CTR measures the engagement level of users with the ads and reflects their interest and response. A higher CTR suggests that the ad is compelling and resonating with the target audience.

- **Return on Investment (ROI):** ROI evaluates the overall financial return generated from the campaign relative to the investment. It is crucial to compare the ROI against the business's desired benchmarks or industry standards to assess campaign performance.

- **Customer Acquisition Cost (CAC):** CAC helps understand the cost associated with acquiring a new customer. It is essential to monitor the CAC in relation to the customer's lifetime value to ensure cost-effectiveness and sustainable growth.

While these metrics are important, it's crucial to consider the specific campaign objectives, industry benchmarks, and the business's unique goals. Additionally, monitoring engagement metrics, such as session duration, bounce rate, and pages per session, can provide insights into user behavior and the effectiveness of the campaign in driving meaningful interactions.

By utilizing tools like Google Ads, Facebook Ads Manager, and affiliate marketing platforms such as ShareASale or CJ Affiliate. With Google Ads and Facebook Ads Manager, you can create targeted pay-per-click (PPC) campaigns, paying only when users click on your ads. By closely monitoring the performance of these campaigns and optimizing them based on conversions and ROI, you can effectively allocate your marketing spend and drive scalable growth. Additionally, by engaging in affiliate marketing, you can collaborate with influencers or partner with publishers who promote your SaaS product, driving more qualified leads and expanding your reach based on measurable outcomes.

By analyzing these metrics and gaining deeper insights into campaign performance, marketers can make informed decisions, optimize strategies, and allocate resources effectively to achieve their goals. It is important to prioritize the metrics aligned with the campaign's objectives and use them collectively to gain a comprehensive understanding of the campaign's impact and success.

11.4 Expanding into New Markets and Verticals

11.4.1 Market Research and Analysis:

Before expanding into new markets or verticals, conduct thorough market research and analysis. Identify target demographics, market trends, and competitive landscapes to assess the viability and potential of new opportunities. By understanding the unique needs and preferences of different markets, you can tailor your marketing strategies and product offerings to maximize success.

Tools like SEMrush, SimilarWeb, and SurveyMonkey can be used for market research and analysis. A SaaS company can utilize SEMrush and SimilarWeb to gain insights into competitors' website traffic, keywords they are targeting, and their overall online presence. This information helps in understanding the competitive landscape and identifying opportunities for differentiation. SurveyMonkey can be employed to conduct surveys and gather customer feedback to understand market needs, preferences, and pain points, enabling the SaaS company to tailor their product offering to meet customer demands.

Real-world example: HubSpot, a leading SaaS company, extensively utilizes market research and analysis tools to understand the marketing industry, identify trends, and deliver relevant content and solutions to their customers. They leverage tools like SEMrush to analyze competitor keywords and SimilarWeb to gain insights into their competitors' website traffic and sources

11.4.2 Localization and Internationalization

When entering new markets, consider localization and internationalization strategies. Adapt your marketing messages, content, and user experience to resonate with the local audience. This includes translating your website, localizing customer support, and considering cultural nuances. By demonstrating a deep understanding of local markets, you can build trust and capture new customer segments effectively.

Tools such as Smartling, Phrase, and Transifex can aid in localization and internationalization efforts. These tools enable SaaS companies to translate their software interfaces, documentation, and marketing materials into different languages, ensuring their product is accessible and appealing to target markets in different regions. They also assist in managing translation workflows, maintaining consistency, and streamlining the localization process.

Real-world example: Slack, a popular SaaS communication platform, successfully expanded into global markets by leveraging localization and internationalization tools. They used Smartling to translate their platform into multiple languages, allowing users worldwide to utilize their services in their preferred language. This approach helped them gain market share and establish a strong global presence.

11.4.3 Strategic Partnerships and Alliances

Forge strategic partnerships and alliances with complementary businesses or industry leaders in your target markets. Collaborations can provide access to new customer bases, enhance brand visibility, and drive growth through shared resources and expertise. By leveraging these partnerships, you can accelerate your expansion efforts and gain a competitive edge.

Tools such as Smartling, Phrase, and Transifex can aid in localization and internationalization efforts. These tools enable SaaS companies to translate their software interfaces, documentation, and marketing materials into different languages, ensuring their product is accessible and appealing to target markets in different regions. They also assist in managing translation workflows, maintaining consistency, and streamlining the localization process.

By utilizing these tools and examples, SaaS companies can effectively conduct market research, expand into new markets, localize their product offerings, and forge strategic partnerships to drive growth and success.

11.5 Managing Growth Challenges and Opportunities

11.5.1 Scalable Infrastructure:

Ensure your SaaS infrastructure is capable of supporting rapid growth. Scale your servers, databases, and networks to handle increased user demands without compromising performance or user experience. Consider cloud-based solutions and scalable technologies that can accommodate growing customer bases and evolving market needs.

Tools like Amazon Web Services (AWS), Microsoft Azure, and Google Cloud Platform provide scalable infrastructure solutions for SaaS companies. These cloud service providers offer reliable and flexible computing resources, storage, and networking capabilities. SaaS companies can leverage these tools to scale their infrastructure as their customer base grows, ensuring high performance and availability for their software applications.

Real-world example: Dropbox, a cloud storage and file-sharing SaaS company, relies on scalable infrastructure provided by AWS. By utilizing AWS's cloud services, Dropbox can handle massive amounts of data storage and deliver a seamless user experience to millions of users worldwide.

11.5.2 Customer Success and Retention:

As your customer base expands, prioritize customer success and retention. Implement robust onboarding processes, provide exceptional customer support, and continuously engage with your customers to ensure their success and satisfaction. By fostering strong relationships and delivering value to your existing customers, you can drive customer retention, promote positive word-of-mouth, and fuel organic growth.

Tools such as customer relationship management (CRM) software, customer support platforms, and analytics tools help SaaS companies drive customer success and retention. CRM platforms like Salesforce or HubSpot allow SaaS companies to manage customer relationships, track customer interactions, and identify opportunities for upselling or cross-selling. Customer support platforms like Zendesk or Intercom enable efficient communication and issue resolution, leading to better customer satisfaction and retention. Analytics tools like Mixpanel or Google Analytics provide insights into user behavior, allowing SaaS companies to proactively address customer needs and enhance their experience.

Real-world example: Zendesk, a customer service software company, utilizes its own customer support platform to provide exceptional customer experiences. They leverage their ticketing system, knowledge base, and live chat features to ensure timely and personalized support, leading to high customer satisfaction and retention rates.

11.5.3 Agile and Adaptive Culture:

Embrace an agile and adaptive culture within your organization. Encourage innovation, experimentation, and continuous improvement. Stay ahead of market trends, monitor customer feedback, and adapt your strategies and offerings accordingly. By fostering a culture that embraces change and embraces new opportunities, you can effectively navigate growth challenges and seize emerging possibilities.

While not specific tools, fostering an agile and adaptive culture within a SaaS company is crucial for success. This involves promoting cross-functional collaboration, continuous learning, and embracing change. Project management and collaboration tools like Jira or Asana facilitate agile methodologies, allowing teams to collaborate, plan, and adapt quickly. Communication and collaboration platforms like Slack or Microsoft Teams foster real-time communication, transparency, and knowledge sharing, supporting an agile and adaptive work culture.

Real-world example: Atlassian, a leading SaaS company known for its project management tools, embraces an agile and adaptive culture. They use their own product, Jira, to manage their internal projects and collaborate across teams. By fostering an environment that encourages innovation, adaptability, and continuous improvement, Atlassian has been able to stay ahead in a rapidly evolving industry.

By utilizing scalable infrastructure, focusing on customer success and retention, and fostering an agile and adaptive culture, SaaS companies can position themselves for growth, deliver exceptional customer experiences, and remain competitive in dynamic market environments.

In conclusion, scaling and achieving sustainable growth in the SaaS industry require a strategic approach and the ability to adapt to changing market dynamics. This chapter has provided valuable insights and actionable strategies for scaling SaaS marketing efforts, expanding into new markets and verticals, and effectively managing growth challenges and opportunities.

By leveraging data-driven decision-making, marketing automation, and performance marketing strategies, SaaS companies can optimize their marketing efforts and drive scalable growth. Market research and analysis, along with localization and strategic partnerships, are essential for successful expansion into new markets and verticals. Additionally, managing growth challenges requires a focus on scalable infrastructure, customer success and retention, and cultivating an agile and adaptive culture.

To achieve long-term success, SaaS businesses must continuously assess their key performance indicators, utilize metrics and analytics tools, and conduct A/B testing to optimize their marketing campaigns. By staying abreast of emerging technologies and trends, SaaS companies can position themselves for future success in an ever-evolving industry.

By studying real-life examples of successful SaaS marketing campaigns and learning from industry leaders and innovators, SaaS businesses can gain valuable insights and apply best practices to their own strategies. Case studies provide practical demonstrations of effective marketing techniques and serve as a source of inspiration for achieving growth and success.

As the SaaS landscape continues to evolve, it is crucial for businesses to remain agile, adaptable, and customer-focused. By embracing the strategies and approaches discussed in this chapter, SaaS companies can position themselves for long-term scalability, sustained growth, and a competitive edge in the market.

Notes

Chapter 12

FUTURE TRENDS IN SAAS MARKETING

The landscape of SaaS marketing is constantly evolving, driven by advancements in technology and changing customer expectations. In this chapter, we will explore the future trends in SaaS marketing, including the impact of emerging technologies and provide predictions and insights into the future of SaaS marketing. By staying ahead of these trends, SaaS businesses can position themselves for success and remain competitive in the ever-evolving market.

12.1 Emerging Technologies and Their Impact on SaaS Marketing

12.1.1 Artificial Intelligence (AI) and Machine Learning:

AI and machine learning are revolutionizing SaaS marketing by enabling businesses to analyze vast amounts of data, personalize customer experiences, and automate repetitive tasks. SaaS companies like Salesforce Einstein, which leverages AI to provide predictive analytics and AI-powered insights, and HubSpot, which utilizes machine learning algorithms to optimize lead scoring and email personalization, are leading the way in harnessing these technologies for enhanced marketing efforts.

12.1.2 Voice Search and Virtual Assistants:

With the rise of voice-activated devices and virtual assistants, voice search is becoming increasingly important in SaaS marketing. SaaS companies like Amazon's Alexa, Google Assistant, and Microsoft's Cortana are at the forefront of voice-enabled technology. SaaS businesses can optimize their content and develop voice-enabled applications to cater to this growing trend, ensuring their products and services are accessible through voice commands.

12.1.3 Augmented Reality (AR) and Virtual Reality (VR):

AR and VR have the potential to transform the way SaaS products are marketed and experienced. SaaS companies like Spatial, which provides virtual collaboration spaces using AR, and Unity, a leading platform for creating immersive experiences, are utilizing these technologies to enhance the customer journey. By allowing users to visualize and interact with products in a virtual environment, SaaS businesses can provide more engaging demonstrations and simulations, increasing customer engagement and driving conversions.

12.1.4 Internet of Things (IoT):

The Internet of Things (IoT) is driving new possibilities for SaaS marketing. SaaS companies like SmartThings, which offers a platform to connect and control IoT devices, and Salesforce IoT Cloud, which enables businesses to capture and analyze IoT data for personalized marketing campaigns, are leveraging IoT to deliver tailored experiences and drive customer engagement. By integrating IoT data into their marketing strategies, SaaS businesses can create targeted messaging and offer personalized solutions based on real-time insights.

12.1.5 Blockchain Technology:

Blockchain technology is disrupting various industries, including SaaS marketing. SaaS companies like Storj, which provides decentralized cloud storage using blockchain, and Brave, a privacy-focused browser that uses blockchain to reward users for their attention, are exploring the potential of blockchain in improving data security, transparency, and user privacy. By leveraging blockchain technology, SaaS businesses can enhance trust and credibility in their marketing efforts, particularly in industries where data privacy and security are paramount.

12.1.6 Chatbots and Conversational Marketing:

Chatbots and conversational marketing platforms are transforming the way SaaS companies engage with customers. SaaS businesses like Intercom, which offers a chatbot platform for customer support and lead generation, and Drift, a conversational marketing platform, are using these technologies to provide personalized interactions, automate customer service, and generate leads. By integrating chatbots and conversational marketing into their strategies, SaaS businesses can deliver real-time support and seamless user experiences.

12.1.7 Predictive Analytics:

Predictive analytics is empowering SaaS companies to anticipate customer behavior, optimize marketing campaigns, and drive better results. SaaS companies like Marketo, which provides predictive analytics for lead scoring and targeting, and Adobe Analytics, which offers advanced analytics and predictive modeling, are utilizing these capabilities to deliver data-driven marketing strategies. By leveraging predictive analytics, SaaS businesses can optimize their targeting, personalize messaging, and improve overall marketing performance.

12.1.8 Cloud Computing:

Cloud computing has revolutionized the SaaS industry by providing scalable and flexible infrastructure for software delivery. SaaS companies like Salesforce, which offers its CRM platform through the cloud, and Dropbox, a cloud-based file storage and collaboration service, rely on cloud computing to deliver their services to customers. By leveraging cloud computing, SaaS businesses can ensure high availability, scalability, and cost-efficiency for their software solutions.

12.1.9 Geolocation Targeting:

Geolocation targeting enables SaaS companies to deliver personalized experiences based on a user's location. SaaS businesses like Uber, which uses geolocation to connect riders with drivers in their vicinity, and Yelp, which provides personalized recommendations based on a user's location, are leveraging geolocation targeting to enhance their marketing efforts. By tailoring messaging and offers to specific locations, SaaS businesses can deliver more relevant and localized experiences to their target audience.

12.1.10 Gamification:

Gamification techniques are being employed by SaaS companies to increase engagement and drive user behavior. SaaS businesses like Duolingo, a language-learning platform that incorporates gamified elements to motivate users, and Fitbit, which gamifies fitness tracking and encourages users to achieve daily goals, are utilizing gamification to enhance their marketing strategies. By incorporating game-like features, challenges, and rewards, SaaS companies can create interactive and engaging experiences that encourage user participation and loyalty.

In the near future, we may witness a convergence of these technologies, where SaaS offerings incorporate a combination of AI, cloud computing, and other emerging technologies. This convergence has the potential to unlock even more powerful capabilities and drive innovation in SaaS marketing. Imagine AI-powered SaaS solutions running on highly scalable cloud infrastructure, enabling advanced analytics, real-time personalization, and seamless user experiences.

While the realization of this combination might seem distant, the possibilities are intriguing. As AI continues to advance and cloud computing becomes more pervasive, we can expect a future where SaaS companies harness the full potential of these technologies to provide highly personalized, intelligent, and efficient solutions.

In conclusion, emerging technologies such as AI, cloud computing, and others are shaping the future of SaaS marketing. SaaS companies are leveraging these technologies to enhance customer experiences, deliver personalized solutions, and drive business growth. The combination of AI and cloud computing holds tremendous potential for the SaaS industry, even though its realization may be far away. As the industry evolves, we can anticipate the emergence of AI-powered SaaS offerings running on robust cloud infrastructure, offering a powerful combination of capabilities to meet the evolving needs of customers in the marketplace.

12.2 Predictions and Insights into the Future of SaaS Marketing

12.2.1 Personalization at Scale:

As customer expectations continue to evolve, personalization has become increasingly crucial in SaaS marketing. The future of SaaS marketing lies in delivering highly personalized experiences at scale. By leveraging data, AI, and automation, SaaS businesses can tailor their marketing messages, recommendations, and offers to individual customers, fostering deeper connections and driving customer loyalty. Several leading SaaS companies have already embraced personalization to provide unique and tailored experiences for their users. Let's explore some real-life examples of how these companies implement personalization at scale in their marketing strategies:

- **Netflix** utilizes user data to personalize recommendations for each viewer, delivering a personalized content discovery experience based on a user's viewing history, preferences, and interactions.

- **Spotify** creates personalized playlists and recommendations based on a user's listening habits, favorite genres, and artists, offering a unique mix of songs in their "Discover Weekly" playlist.

- **Amazon** uses personalization extensively by recommending products based on a customer's browsing and purchase history, providing personalized recommendations on the homepage, product pages, and through targeted email campaigns.

- **HubSpot** delivers personalized email marketing campaigns based on a user's engagement history, interests, and behavior, nurturing leads and guiding them through the buyer's journey.

- **Adobe's** marketing automation platform enables businesses to create personalized experiences across multiple channels, utilizing features like dynamic content and personalization based on user segments.

- **Evergage** offers real-time personalization tools that allow SaaS companies to deliver tailored experiences on their websites and applications, including personalized product recommendations and dynamic content based on user behavior.

- **Salesforce**'s AI-powered marketing cloud, Einstein, leverages customer data and machine learning to deliver personalized marketing campaigns, predict customer behavior, and recommend next best actions.

- **Shopify** empowers businesses to create personalized shopping experiences using customization options for product recommendations, email marketing, and personalized storefronts based on user preferences.

- **Mailchimp** enables businesses to send personalized email marketing campaigns by segmenting subscribers based on behavior, demographics, and preferences, delivering targeted messages and improving engagement.

- **Netflix** also personalizes its email communications, sending customized emails based on a user's viewing history and preferences to encourage them to continue watching their favorite shows or discover new ones.

These examples showcase how SaaS companies leverage personalization techniques, data analysis, and automation to provide highly tailored experiences to their customers. By harnessing customer data and leveraging technology, these companies aim to establish deeper connections, drive engagement, and cultivate long-term customer loyalty at scale.

12.2.2 User-Generated Content (UGC)

User-generated content, including reviews, testimonials, and social media posts, holds immense value in SaaS marketing. As customers increasingly seek authentic experiences shared by their peers, the role of user-generated content becomes pivotal. SaaS businesses can capitalize on the power of UGC by actively encouraging and amplifying user-generated content, leveraging social proof to establish trust and influence potential customers' purchasing decisions. Let's explore real-life examples of how leading SaaS companies harness the potential of user-generated content in their marketing strategies:

- **Airbnb** encourages users to share their travel experiences through reviews and testimonials. These authentic stories help build trust among potential travellers and influence their booking decisions.

- **Yelp** relies heavily on user-generated reviews to provide insights and recommendations for local businesses. By showcasing genuine customer experiences, Yelp helps users make informed decisions about where to dine, shop, or seek services.

- **Slack** features customer testimonials on their website, showcasing how businesses use their communication platform to enhance productivity and collaboration. These testimonials serve as social proof and inspire confidence in potential customers.

- **TripAdvisor** is renowned for its user-generated travel content, including reviews, photos, and recommendations. The platform leverages this UGC to assist travelers in planning trips and selecting accommodations, activities, and restaurants.

- **Canva** actively encourages users to share their designs on social media and provides a platform for users to showcase their creations. This user-generated content demonstrates the versatility and creativity of Canva's design tools, attracting new users.

- **GoPro** encourages customers to share their adventurous experiences captured with GoPro cameras through the company's social media channels. This UGC not only showcases the product's capabilities but also inspires others to embark on their own adventures.

- **Dropbox** features customer success stories on their website, highlighting how businesses leverage their file-sharing and collaboration platform. These stories serve as powerful testimonials, demonstrating the impact Dropbox has on improving workflows and productivity.

- **Wix** showcases user-created website designs on their platform, allowing customers to share their websites and inspire others. This UGC not only promotes Wix's website-building capabilities but also showcases the diverse range of websites that can be created with their tools.

- **Zendesk** encourages customers to share their support experiences on social media using branded hashtags. This UGC helps build a positive reputation for Zendesk's customer support services and creates a sense of community among users.

- **YouTube** relies heavily on user-generated content in the form of videos uploaded by creators. The platform's success is built on users sharing their expertise, entertainment, and personal experiences, attracting a vast audience and advertisers.

These examples demonstrate how SaaS companies effectively leverage user-generated content to build trust, provide social proof, and influence potential customers. By actively encouraging and amplifying UGC, these companies tap into the authentic voices of their customers, creating a powerful marketing tool that resonates with their target audience.

12.2.3 Data Privacy and Security:

In an era of increasing data privacy concerns, SaaS businesses must prioritize data privacy and security as integral components of their marketing strategies. With heightened awareness among customers regarding the handling of their personal information, transparency, consent management, and secure data practices are crucial for building trust. SaaS marketers need to stay informed about evolving privacy regulations and adopt robust measures to protect customer data. Let's explore real-life examples of how leading SaaS companies address data privacy and security in their marketing efforts:

- **Google** prominently communicates its commitment to data privacy and security, providing transparency about its data collection practices and offering users control over their data through privacy settings. Google's marketing emphasizes secure cloud services and encryption technologies to instill confidence in users.

- **Microsoft** actively promotes its strong data protection measures, including advanced encryption, multi-factor authentication, and compliance with global privacy regulations. Marketing campaigns highlight the company's commitment to securing customer data and maintaining privacy standards.

- **Salesforce** incorporates data privacy and security as key pillars of its marketing messaging. The company emphasizes its compliance with privacy regulations, secure infrastructure, and robust access controls to assure customers that their data is protected.

- **Zoom** addresses data privacy concerns through transparency and proactive security measures. The company publishes detailed information about its security practices, regularly updates its security features, and offers end-to-end encryption options for meetings to safeguard user data.

- **Dropbox** highlights its commitment to data privacy and security through its marketing communications. The company emphasizes secure file storage, encryption, and user controls to ensure that customer data remains protected within its platform.

- **Apple** focuses on user privacy as a key selling point for its products and services. Marketing campaigns highlight features like intelligent tracking prevention, strong device encryption, and app privacy labels to showcase Apple's commitment to safeguarding user data.

- **Shopify** places emphasis on secure e-commerce transactions and data protection in its marketing efforts. The company promotes features such as SSL certificates, secure checkout processes, and adherence to industry-standard security practices to assure customers of their data's safety.

- **LastPass,** a password management tool, emphasizes data security and privacy as core features of its product. Marketing messaging highlights end-to-end encryption, strong password generation, and secure password sharing to alleviate concerns about data vulnerability.

- **McAfee,** a cybersecurity company, centers its marketing around protecting user data from online threats. The company offers a suite of security solutions, including antivirus software, identity theft protection, and secure browsing features, to address data privacy concerns.

- **ProtonMail,** an encrypted email service provider, positions itself as a secure alternative to traditional email providers. Marketing campaigns highlight end-to-end encryption, zero-access architecture, and protection against surveillance to appeal to users who prioritize data privacy.

These examples showcase how leading SaaS companies address data privacy and security in their marketing strategies. By emphasizing transparency, consent management, and robust data protection measures, these companies aim to build trust with their customers and alleviate concerns about data privacy. Prioritizing data privacy and staying updated on evolving privacy regulations are essential for SaaS marketers to maintain the trust and confidence of their user base.

The future of SaaS marketing is filled with exciting possibilities. Emerging technologies like AI, voice search, AR, and VR are reshaping the way SaaS products are marketed and experienced. By embracing these trends and staying ahead of the curve, SaaS businesses can adapt their strategies, enhance customer experiences, and achieve long-term success in the dynamic world of SaaS marketing.

Chapter 13

CASE STUDIES AND EXAMPLES

In this chapter, we will dive into real-life case studies and examples of successful SaaS marketing campaigns. By examining the strategies and tactics employed by industry leaders and innovators, we can gain valuable insights and learn from their experiences. These case studies will showcase the power of effective SaaS marketing and provide inspiration for businesses looking to elevate their marketing efforts.

13.1 Real-Life Examples of Successful SaaS Marketing Campaigns

13.1.1 Slack: Revolutionizing Team Collaboration

Slack's marketing campaign focused on addressing the pain points of team collaboration and positioned their product as the ultimate solution. By leveraging content marketing, social media, and referral programs, Slack gained widespread adoption and became a household name in the SaaS industry. We will delve into the key strategies that propelled Slack's success and explore the lessons we can learn from their innovative marketing approaches like

- **Content Marketing:** Slack invested in creating valuable and informative content that addressed the pain points and challenges associated with team collaboration. This content included blog posts, whitepapers, case studies, and how-to guides. By sharing this content, Slack established itself as an authority in the field and attracted a relevant audience.

- **Social Media Engagement:** Slack actively engaged with its audience on social media platforms. They used platforms like Twitter, LinkedIn, and Facebook to share updates, interact with users, and showcase customer success stories. This approach helped them build a strong online community and foster customer loyalty.

- **Referral Programs:** Slack introduced referral programs that encouraged their existing users to invite others to join the platform. Incentives, such as extended free trials or discounts, motivated users to spread the word about Slack. This strategy led to rapid user acquisition and growth.

- **User-Centric Design:** Slack's user interface and experience were designed with the end user in mind. The platform's intuitive design made it easy for teams to adopt Slack quickly and integrate it into their workflows, increasing user satisfaction and adoption rates.

- **Freemium Model:** Slack initially offered a freemium model, allowing teams to use the platform for free with limitations. This approach allowed users to experience the value of Slack before committing to a paid plan, which was a significant driver of adoption.

- **Partnerships and Integrations:** Slack actively sought partnerships with other software and service providers to expand its ecosystem. This allowed users to integrate Slack with other tools they were already using, making Slack an even more valuable part of their daily work.

- **Community Building:** Slack fostered a sense of community among its users. This included hosting events, webinars, and user groups to encourage knowledge sharing and networking among its user base.

- **Innovative Branding and Voice:** Slack developed a unique brand identity and voice, characterized by humor and approachability. This set them apart from more traditional corporate communication tools and made them more appealing to a broader audience.

- **Continuous Improvement:** Slack regularly updated and improved its platform based on user feedback. This commitment to user satisfaction and product refinement ensured long-term success.

- **Data-Driven Decision-Making**: Slack relied on data and analytics to make informed decisions about its marketing campaigns, user engagement, and product development. This data-driven approach allowed them to iterate and optimize their strategies.

The combination of content marketing, social media engagement, referral programs, and user-centric design, along with a unique brand identity and a commitment to continuous improvement, helped Slack become a leader in the team collaboration and SaaS industry.

13.1.2 HubSpot: Inbound Marketing Mastery

HubSpot's inbound marketing strategy has been widely recognized for its effectiveness. Through content creation, SEO optimization, and lead nurturing, HubSpot attracted a massive audience and positioned itself as a thought leader in the marketing automation space. We will examine HubSpot's inbound marketing journey, highlighting the key tactics that contributed to their success and how they leveraged their own product to drive customer acquisition.

- **Content Creation:** HubSpot's success in inbound marketing was built on a foundation of high-quality content. They consistently produced blog posts, ebooks, webinars, and other informative content that addressed the pain points and challenges faced by their target audience. This content not only showcased their expertise but also drew in a significant and engaged audience.

- **SEO Optimization:** HubSpot recognized the importance of search engine optimization (SEO) in attracting organic traffic. They optimized their content and website to rank well in search engines, ensuring that their valuable content was discoverable by those actively searching for solutions in the marketing and automation space.

- **Lead Nurturing:** HubSpot excelled in lead nurturing, leveraging marketing automation tools to engage and educate potential customers. They implemented email marketing campaigns, drip sequences, and personalized content recommendations to guide leads through the sales funnel. This approach helped build strong customer relationships and drive conversions.

- **Positioning as a Thought Leader:** HubSpot didn't just market their product; they positioned themselves as thought leaders and educators in the field of marketing automation. Their blog, resources, and industry reports provided valuable insights and established trust and authority within their target market.

- **Leveraging Their Own Product:** HubSpot practiced what they preached by using their own marketing automation tools. They demonstrated the power of their platform by showcasing how it could help other businesses achieve similar marketing success. This not only proved their product's efficacy but also attracted customers looking for marketing automation solutions.

- **Customer Acquisition:** HubSpot's inbound marketing strategy resulted in customer acquisition, as businesses impressed by their content, expertise, and product demonstrations became paying customers. By focusing on inbound techniques, they attracted a highly relevant and qualified customer base.

In summary, HubSpot's inbound marketing mastery was characterized by content creation, SEO optimization, lead nurturing, thought leadership positioning, and the strategic use of their own product. These tactics played a crucial role in their success, making HubSpot a prominent figure in the marketing automation space and showcasing the potential of inbound marketing as an effective customer acquisition strategy that come to the website/channel to find solution or learn more about it and end up using the well-defined templates or free product trail that Hubspot offers.

13.1.3 Canva: Empowering Creativity for All

Canva disrupted the graphic design industry by providing a user-friendly platform that empowers individuals and businesses to create stunning visuals. Their marketing campaign focused on simplicity, accessibility, and the democratization of design. We will explore Canva's growth strategies, including their freemium model, strategic partnerships, and social media marketing, to understand how they captured a vast user base and achieved remarkable success.

- ✔ **Freemium Model:** Canva adopted a freemium model that allowed users to access a wide range of design tools and templates for free. By providing a valuable free tier, Canva attracted a large user base that could explore the platform's capabilities before upgrading to a paid subscription for advanced features. This approach is similar to Slack's freemium model, which we discussed earlier.

- ✔ **Strategic Partnerships:** Canva formed strategic partnerships with companies and organizations to expand its reach and integrate its platform into various industries. For example, they partnered with education institutions to provide educators and students with access to design tools, fostering brand loyalty and creating a future user base.

- ✔ **Social Media Marketing:** Canva leveraged social media effectively to promote its platform. They encouraged users to share their creations on social media, creating a network effect as others discovered Canva through shared content. Additionally, Canva's own social media profiles featured creative user-generated content, demonstrating the platform's versatility and inspiring new users to join.

- **User-Generated Content:** Canva empowered its users to create and share content that showcased the platform's capabilities. This included graphics, presentations, and social media posts designed using Canva. Sharing user success stories and featuring user-generated content on their website and social media channels helped build trust and credibility.

- **Educational Resources:** Canva recognized the value of educating users on design principles and best practices. They created a wealth of educational resources, including blog posts, tutorials, and design courses, which not only improved user skills but also kept users engaged and returning to the platform.

- **Localized Content:** To appeal to a global audience, Canva provided localized content and templates in multiple languages. This approach made the platform accessible to users around the world, further contributing to its impressive user base and international success.

- **Mobile Accessibility:** Canva's mobile app made it easy for users to design on the go, extending their reach beyond desktop users. Mobile accessibility added a new dimension to their user base, attracting those who preferred creating visuals on their smartphones or tablets.

In summary, Canva's success in empowering creativity for all was achieved through a combination of a freemium model, strategic partnerships, social media marketing, user-generated content, educational resources, localized content, and mobile accessibility. These strategies allowed Canva to revolutionize the graphic design industry and attract a diverse and extensive user base.

Chapter 14

Bonus Chapters

SAAS MARKETING MISTAKES AND SOLUTIONS

Free Trials Included

While marketing a SaaS (Software as a Service) product, there are several common mistakes that people make. Here are the top 10 mistakes and their solutions, along with real-world examples:

1. **Lack of Target Audience Understanding:**

   a. **Mistake:** Failing to understand the needs, pain points, and preferences of the target audience.

   b. **Solution:** Conduct thorough market research, create buyer personas, and tailor marketing messages accordingly.

   c. **Example:** HubSpot conducts extensive market research and creates buyer personas to tailor their marketing messages. They offer free tools and resources targeted at different buyer personas to address their specific pain points and challenges.

2. **Weak Value Proposition:**

   a. **Mistake:** Failing to communicate the unique value proposition of the SaaS product effectively.

   b. **Solution:** Clearly articulate the benefits and advantages of the product, emphasizing how it solves customers' problems.

   c. **Example:** Slack effectively communicates its unique value proposition as a collaborative communication tool that eliminates excessive email communication and boosts team productivity.

3. **Inadequate Product Differentiation:**

   a. **Mistake:** Not highlighting the distinctive features or advantages that set the SaaS product apart from competitors.

   b. **Solution:** Identify key differentiators and emphasize them in marketing campaigns.

   c. **Example:** Zoom highlights its user-friendly interface, high-quality video conferencing, and ease of use, setting it apart from other video conferencing platforms.

4. **Poor Content Strategy:**

   a. **Mistake:** Creating low-quality or irrelevant content that fails to engage and educate the target audience.

   b. **Solution:** Develop a well-defined content strategy that aligns with the target audience's interests, pain points, and stage in the buyer's journey.

   c. **Example:** Buffer develops a well-defined content strategy focused on social media marketing. Their blog provides valuable content catering to their target audience's needs

5. **Ignoring Customer Feedback:**

    a. **Mistake:** Neglecting customer feedback and failing to incorporate it into product development and marketing strategies.

    b. **Solution:** Actively listen to customer feedback, address their concerns, and implement necessary improvements.

    c. **Example:** Mailchimp actively listens to customer feedback, addresses concerns, and incorporates necessary improvements into product updates and new feature releases.

6. **Ineffective Pricing Strategy:**

    a. **Mistake:** Setting incorrect pricing or failing to communicate the value for the chosen price point.

    b. **Solution:** Conduct pricing research, analyze market trends, and clearly communicate the value customers will receive at the chosen price.

    c. **Example:** Dropbox implemented a freemium pricing model, allowing users to experience the product's value before committing to a paid plan.

7. **Poor User Onboarding Experience:**

    a. **Mistake:** Overcomplicating the user onboarding process or failing to provide adequate guidance.

    b. **Solution:** Simplify the onboarding process and provide comprehensive resources like tutorials, guides, and videos.

    c. **Example:** Canva offers a seamless onboarding experience with intuitive UI, guided tours, and helpful tips to simplify the user onboarding process.

8. **Neglecting Customer Retention:**

    a. **Mistake:** Focusing solely on acquiring new customers while neglecting existing ones.

    b. **Solution:** Develop a customer retention strategy that includes personalized communication, loyalty programs, and ongoing support.

    c. **Example:** Adobe Creative Cloud focuses on customer retention through regular updates, exclusive features, and discounts for their existing customer base.

9. **Lack of Marketing Analytics:**

    a. **Mistake:** Not tracking and analyzing marketing metrics to assess the effectiveness of campaigns.

    b. **Solution:** Set up robust analytics tools to measure key metrics, such as conversion rates, customer acquisition cost (CAC), and customer lifetime value (CLTV).

    c. **Example:** Google Analytics provides comprehensive data for tracking and analyzing marketing metrics, such as conversion rates, CAC, and CLTV.

10. **Inconsistent Branding:**

    a. **Mistake:** Inconsistent messaging, visual identity, or brand voice across different marketing channels.

    b. **Solution:** Develop brand guidelines and ensure consistent branding across all touchpoints.

    c. **Example:** Slack maintains consistent branding with its distinctive logo, color scheme, and tone of voice, which resonates with its target audience

However, the biggest one I feel is to not offering free trials can indeed be a potential mistake in SaaS marketing. Providing free trials allows potential customers to experience the product firsthand, understand its value, and evaluate its suitability for their needs. Here are some considerations and potential solutions:

- ✔ **Customer Experience:** Free trials enable customers to test the product and get a feel for its features, usability, and benefits. It helps build trust and confidence in the product before committing to a purchase.

- ✔ **Reduced Risk:** Offering a free trial reduces the perceived risk for potential customers. They can try the product without making a financial commitment upfront, increasing the likelihood of conversion.

- ✔ **Competitive Advantage:** In a competitive SaaS market, offering a free trial can give your product an edge over competitors who do not provide this opportunity. It allows you to showcase the value and superiority of your product compared to others.

- ✔ **Lead Generation:** Free trials can serve as effective lead generation tools. By collecting contact information from users who sign up for a trial, you can nurture those leads and convert them into paying customers through targeted marketing efforts.

- ✔ **Upselling and Cross-selling:** During the free trial period, you can highlight premium features or offer additional services that users can upgrade to. This provides an opportunity to upsell or cross-sell, increasing revenue potential.

Of course, there may be situations where offering a free trial may not be suitable for every SaaS product. Some factors to consider include the complexity of the product, cost implications, and the nature of the target audience. However, in many cases, offering a free trial can be a valuable strategy to attract, engage, and convert potential customers.

Finding the true Valuation of your SaaS Offering

Determining the true valuation of a Software-as-a-Service (SaaS) offering involves a comprehensive analysis of various factors. While the process can be complex and may require assistance from professionals such as financial advisors or valuation experts, here are some general steps to help you get started:

1. **Understand your business model:** Gain a deep understanding of your SaaS business model, including revenue streams, customer acquisition and retention strategies, pricing structure, and growth projections. This foundational knowledge will help you assess the value of your offering accurately.

    a. Identify your SaaS revenue streams:

        i. **Subscription fees:** This is a common revenue stream where customers pay a recurring fee (monthly or annually) to access your SaaS product or services.

        ii. **Usage-based pricing:** Some SaaS companies charge customers based on their actual usage or consumption of the software. For example, a cloud storage provider may charge based on the amount of data stored or the number of API calls made.

        iii. **Add-on services:** You can offer additional services or features that complement your core SaaS product. These can be premium features, consulting services, customization options, or integrations with other tools.

        iv. **Implementation fees:** In certain cases, you may charge customers an upfront fee for setting up and implementing your SaaS solution, especially if it requires significant onboarding or configuration.

b. Analyze your customer acquisition and retention strategies:

    i. **Inbound marketing:** If you rely on inbound marketing, you attract customers through content marketing, search engine optimization (SEO), social media, or referrals. Analyze the effectiveness of your inbound marketing efforts in terms of lead generation and conversion rates.

    ii. **Partnerships:** Assess if you have strategic partnerships with other companies to acquire customers. These can be reseller partnerships, affiliate programs, or integration partnerships that expand your reach and customer base.

    iii. **Direct sales:** Determine if your sales team engages in direct sales efforts to reach and acquire customers. This involves proactive outreach, product demos, negotiations, and closing deals.

    iv. **Customer churn reduction:** Churn refers to the rate at which customers cancel or stop using your SaaS product. Analyze your customer churn and identify strategies to reduce it. This may involve improving customer onboarding, enhancing product features, offering exceptional customer support, or implementing customer success programs to ensure customer satisfaction and long-term retention.

2. By **understanding your revenue streams** and analyzing customer concentration and retention strategies, you gain insights into the financial stability and growth potential of your SaaS offering. These factors contribute to the overall valuation of your business.

    a. **Customer Concentration**: Customer Concentration refers to the extent to which your SaaS company's revenue is dependent on a small number of customers. It helps assess the risk associated with relying heavily on a few key clients. To determine the customer concentration, you need to identify the percentage of revenue contributed by your top customers, typically the top five customers. Here's an example to illustrate this: Suppose your SaaS company generates $1 million in total revenue, and out of that, $700,000 comes from a single enterprise client, while the remaining $300,000 is distributed across other customers. In this case, your customer concentration is 70% ($700,000 / $1,000,000). A high customer concentration suggests that your revenue is highly dependent on a small number of clients, which can pose risks if one or more of those clients reduce their business or decide to switch providers.

b. **Customer Retention Rate:** Customer Retention Rate measures the percentage of customers who renew their subscriptions or continue to use your SaaS product over a specific period. It is an essential metric for evaluating the loyalty and satisfaction of your customer base. To calculate the customer retention rate, you need to compare the number of customers at the end of a given period (e.g., a month or a year) with the number of customers you had at the beginning of that period. Here's an example to illustrate this: If you started with 100 customers and, by the end of the year, you still have 80 customers, your customer retention rate would be 80% (80 customers / 100 customers). A high customer retention rate indicates that your customers are satisfied with your product, leading to a stable revenue stream and potential for upselling and expansion within your existing customer base.

Both Customer Concentration and Customer Retention Rate provide insights into the stability and growth potential of your business:

- High customer concentration can be risky if you heavily rely on a small number of clients, as losing one or more of them could significantly impact your revenue.

- A high customer retention rate indicates customer satisfaction and loyalty, reducing the need for constant acquisition of new customers and fostering long-term revenue growth.

Considering these factors alongside other aspects of your business will contribute to a more comprehensive understanding of your SaaS offering's valuation.

3. **Analyze financial metrics:** Evaluate key financial metrics such as annual recurring revenue (ARR), monthly recurring revenue (MRR), customer acquisition cost (CAC), customer lifetime value (CLTV), gross margin, and churn rate. These metrics provide insights into your revenue generation, profitability, and scalability, which are critical for valuation.

- **Annual Recurring Revenue (ARR):** ARR is a key financial metric that represents the total annual revenue generated by your SaaS company from subscription fees. It excludes one-time or non-recurring revenue sources. To illustrate this, let's consider an example:

  Suppose your SaaS company generates $1 million in recurring revenue from subscription fees. This means that over a 12-month period, you have contracts in place that generate $1 million in revenue.

- **Customer Acquisition Cost (CAC):** CAC measures the average cost incurred by your SaaS company to acquire a new customer. It includes various expenses related to sales and marketing efforts. To calculate CAC, you divide the total sales and marketing expenses by the number of new customers acquired within a specific time frame. For instance:

  If your sales and marketing expenses amount to $500,000, and you acquired 100 new customers during that period, your CAC would be $5,000 ($500,000 / 100).

- **Customer Lifetime Value (CLTV):** CLTV represents the average revenue that a customer generates throughout their relationship with your company. It helps you understand the long-term value each customer brings to your business. To calculate CLTV, you multiply the average revenue per customer by the average customer lifespan. Here's an example:

  If, on average, each customer pays $1,000 per year and remains a customer for five years, the CLTV would be $5,000 ($1,000 x 5).

Analyzing these metrics provides valuable insights into your business's financial performance and growth potential:

- High ARR indicates a strong revenue base and stability in your recurring revenue streams.

- Monitoring CAC is crucial to ensure that your customer acquisition costs are reasonable and sustainable, allowing you to achieve profitability.

- CLTV helps you understand the revenue potential of each customer and can guide decisions regarding customer acquisition and retention strategies.

By considering these metrics alongside other factors like market opportunity, customer base, and growth potential, you can better assess the valuation of your SaaS offering and make informed decisions about your business strategy. (Any investor might ask for these numbers from you before investing)

4. **Assess market opportunity**: Determine the size and growth potential of your target market. Conduct market research to gather data on industry trends, competitive landscape, and customer demand. A larger and rapidly expanding market can positively impact your valuation.

   Let's understand what is Total Addressable Market (TAM) and Market Growth Rate:

   - **Total Addressable Market (TAM):** The Total Addressable Market represents the total revenue opportunity available for a particular product or service within a specific market. It is an estimation of the maximum potential market size for a given offering. To determine the TAM, you need to estimate the size of the relevant market segment that your SaaS product serves. For example, if you're offering HR software, you would estimate the size of the global HR software market. This can be done by conducting market research, analyzing industry reports, or consulting reputable sources to gather data on the market size. By estimating the TAM, you can gauge the revenue potential of your SaaS offering within the broader market.

- **Market Growth Rate:** The Market Growth Rate refers to the projected rate at which a specific market segment or industry is expected to grow over a certain period. It provides insights into the future prospects and opportunities for companies operating within that market. To understand the Market Growth Rate, you need to research and analyze industry reports, market studies, and expert forecasts to identify the expected growth rate of the market segment in which your SaaS offering operates. For example, if you're offering HR software, you would research the projected growth rate of the HR software market.

Comparing the Market Growth Rate of your specific market segment with other segments can provide valuable insights for your SaaS offering:

A higher Market Growth Rate indicates a rapidly expanding market with increasing demand, presenting potential opportunities for revenue growth and market share capture.

Comparing the growth rate of your market segment to other segments helps you understand the relative growth potential and attractiveness of your specific market.

By considering the Total Addressable Market and the Market Growth Rate, you can assess the size of the market opportunity for your SaaS offering and evaluate its growth prospects. These factors are important considerations when determining the valuation and future potential of your business

5. **Compare with industry benchmarks**: Research and compare your SaaS offering with similar companies in your industry. Look for publicly available information or consult industry reports to understand how your performance and growth metrics stack up against industry benchmarks. This analysis can help you gauge your relative valuation.

   To research industry reports or public filings and identify comparable SaaS companies, as well as to find relevant financial metrics, you can follow these steps:

Identify relevant industry reports: Look for industry-specific reports or studies that provide insights into the SaaS market or specific segments within the industry. These reports often include market trends, growth forecasts, and financial performance data of key players. Some sources for industry reports include:

- **Market research firms:** Companies like Gartner, Forrester Research, IDC, and Statista often publish industry reports, market analyses, and forecasts. While some reports may require a subscription or purchase, they often offer free excerpts or summaries.

- **Trade publications:** Industry-specific publications or online magazines may provide articles, research, or reports on the SaaS sector, including financial metrics and performance benchmarks.

- **Search public filings like Annual reports:** Publicly-traded SaaS companies are required to file annual reports (such as Form 10-K in the United States) with regulatory authorities. These reports provide comprehensive financial information, including revenue metrics, growth rates, and operational details. These filings can be accessed through the Securities and Exchange Commission (SEC) website in the U.S. or the relevant regulatory authority in other countries.

Explore free financial data sources:

- **Company websites:** Visit the websites of SaaS companies, especially those in your industry or with a similar business model. They often provide investor relations sections or financial reports that highlight key financial metrics and performance indicators.

- **News and press releases:** Keep an eye on news articles and press releases related to SaaS companies. They may provide insights into financial milestones, funding rounds, or performance metrics.

- **Public databases:** Platforms like Crunchbase or PitchBook aggregate data on companies, including SaaS providers. While not all financial information may be available for free, these platforms can provide some high-level metrics and funding details.

When benchmarking your performance against comparable SaaS companies, you can use the financial metrics you gather, such as ARR (Annual Recurring Revenue), MRR (Monthly Recurring Revenue), and churn rate, to assess how your business measures up in terms of revenue generation, growth rates, and customer retention. Compare these metrics with those of similar companies to identify areas of strength or areas that may require improvement.

Remember to exercise caution and verify the reliability and accuracy of the sources you use for research. Professional financial databases or consulting services can provide more comprehensive and accurate data but may involve subscription fees.

6. **Consider technology and intellectual property:** Assess the uniqueness and defensibility of your technology, intellectual property (IP), and proprietary assets. Patents, trademarks, copyrights, and trade secrets can enhance your valuation by providing a competitive advantage and barriers to entry for potential competitors.

   Let's delve into the explanations of evaluating proprietary technology and assessing intellectual property rights:

   - **Evaluate proprietary technology**: Proprietary technology refers to unique algorithms, innovative features, or any distinctive technological aspects that set your SaaS offering apart from competitors. When evaluating proprietary technology, you assess the value and potential impact it brings to your business, which can influence its valuation. Here's how this evaluation can affect your SaaS offering:

   - **Unique algorithm:** If your SaaS solution incorporates a proprietary algorithm that delivers superior performance, efficiency, or accuracy compared to existing alternatives, it can increase the value of your offering.

- **Innovative features:** If your SaaS product introduces innovative features or functionalities that solve specific pain points for customers or provide a competitive edge, it can enhance the valuation by attracting more users and generating differentiation in the market.

- **Assess intellectual property rights**: Intellectual property (IP) rights protect the intangible assets of your SaaS solution and can contribute to its valuation. Assessing intellectual property rights involves determining if your SaaS offering is protected by patents, trademarks, copyrights, or trade secrets. Here's how these different forms of IP protection can impact your valuation:

- **Patents:** If you have obtained patents for unique technologies or processes within your SaaS offering, it can provide a strong competitive advantage, potentially increasing the valuation. Patents offer legal protection against others using, making, or selling your patented inventions.

- **Trademarks:** Trademarks protect your brand name, logos, or slogans associated with your SaaS offering. Having strong and recognizable trademarks can enhance your brand value and potentially increase its valuation.

- **Copyrights:** Copyright protection applies to original creative works, such as software code, design elements, or written content. Copyrights provide legal protection against unauthorized copying or distribution of your SaaS product, contributing to its valuation.

- **Trade secrets:** Trade secrets refer to confidential information that gives your SaaS offering a competitive advantage. This can include proprietary algorithms, customer lists, or undisclosed business processes. Protecting trade secrets through non-disclosure agreements (NDAs) and robust security measures can increase the valuation by safeguarding your unique knowledge and advantage.

Evaluating proprietary technology and assessing intellectual property rights helps identify the unique and protected aspects of your SaaS offering, which can positively impact its valuation. These factors demonstrate differentiation, market potential, and barriers to entry for competitors.

7. **Factor in growth potential:** Present a compelling growth story to potential investors or acquirers. Highlight your product roadmap, expansion plans, and strategies for scaling the business. Demonstrating a clear path to future growth can positively impact your valuation.

   Let's delve into the explanations of presenting a detailed product roadmap and highlighting expansion plans:

   - **Present a detailed product roadmap:** A product roadmap outlines the future direction, features, and enhancements planned for your SaaS offering. It provides a strategic overview of how your product will evolve over time to meet customer needs and drive user adoption and revenue growth. When presenting a detailed product roadmap, you are showcasing the planned development and improvements, which can positively impact the valuation of your SaaS offering. Here's how it can affect your valuation:

   - **User adoption:** Demonstrating a clear roadmap with exciting and valuable features can attract new users and increase user adoption, indicating the growth potential of your user base and revenue.

   - **Revenue growth:** Highlighting upcoming enhancements or premium features can create opportunities for upselling or increasing subscription pricing, leading to revenue growth potential.

   - **Competitive advantage:** A product roadmap that showcases innovative and unique features or addresses key market needs can differentiate your SaaS offering from competitors, increasing its value in the eyes of potential investors or acquirers.

- **Highlight expansion plans:** Expansion plans refer to strategies and initiatives aimed at entering new geographic markets or verticals to scale the business beyond its current boundaries. When highlighting expansion plans, you showcase the potential for further growth and revenue diversification. Here's how it can impact the valuation of your SaaS offering:

- **Market potential:** Identifying new geographic markets or underserved verticals with high demand for your SaaS offering demonstrates the size of the untapped market opportunity, which can positively influence the valuation.

- **Scalability:** Expansion plans that showcase the ability to replicate success in new markets or verticals indicate the scalability of your business model, which can attract investors or acquirers seeking growth potential.

- **Diversification:** Targeting new markets or verticals reduces reliance on a single market segment, enhancing the stability and long-term viability of your SaaS offering, thereby impacting its valuation positively.

By presenting a detailed product roadmap and highlighting expansion plans, you provide a clear vision for the future growth and development of your SaaS offering. These factors demonstrate your ability to evolve, adapt to market needs, and seize opportunities, which can increase the valuation by showcasing the potential for continued revenue growth and market expansion.

8. **Seek expert advice**: Engage with professionals who specialize in valuations, such as financial advisors or valuation experts with experience in the SaaS industry. They can provide a more accurate assessment by applying sophisticated valuation methodologies and considering factors specific to the SaaS sector.

Here's some guidance on finding and hiring such professionals, their qualifications, the time it takes for valuation, and how valuation can increase over time:

Finding and hiring a financial advisor or valuation expert:

- **Research:** Conduct thorough research online, check industry directories, or seek referrals from trusted sources within the SaaS industry. Look for professionals or firms that specialize in business valuation, particularly with experience in valuing SaaS companies.

- **Qualifications:** Seek individuals or firms with relevant qualifications, such as Certified Valuation Analyst (CVA), Chartered Financial Analyst (CFA), or Accredited Senior Appraiser (ASA) designations. Additionally, consider their experience working with SaaS businesses and their understanding of the industry dynamics.

- **Interviews and references:** Interview potential advisors or experts to understand their approach, expertise, and track record. Request references or case studies from past clients in the SaaS sector to assess their competence and ability to deliver accurate valuations.

- **Time for valuation:** The time required for a valuation depends on various factors, including the complexity of your SaaS business, the availability of financial data, and the scope of the valuation engagement. It typically involves a detailed analysis of financial statements, market research, industry benchmarking, and other relevant considerations. Valuations can range from several weeks to a couple of months, depending on the specific circumstances.

**********_**Valuation increases over time**_*********

The valuation of a SaaS offering can increase over time based on various factors, such as:

- **Revenue growth:** If your SaaS company demonstrates consistent revenue growth and positive financial performance, it can contribute to a higher valuation.

- **Market expansion:** Successfully entering new markets, reaching new customer segments, or expanding your product offerings can enhance the valuation by increasing the growth potential and market reach.

- **Intellectual property development:** Developing and protecting intellectual property, such as proprietary technology or patents, can strengthen the competitive advantage and valuation of your SaaS offering.

- **Operational efficiency:** Improving operational efficiency, reducing costs, or increasing profit margins can positively impact the valuation.

It's important to note that valuation can also fluctuate based on market conditions, industry trends, and other external factors. Engaging a financial advisor or valuation expert can help you navigate these dynamics and provide up-to-date insights on the valuation of your SaaS offering.

Remember, the valuation process is complex, and the steps mentioned here provide a general framework. The specific circumstances of your SaaS offering may require additional considerations and tailored approaches.

HOW TO RAISE MONEY FOR YOUR SAAS IDEA

Launching and scaling a Software-as-a-Service (SaaS) business often requires significant capital investment. To raise money for your SaaS idea, it is essential to understand the fundraising landscape and develop a strategic approach. This chapter will outline the steps you can take to raise funds for your SaaS startup, along with detailed explanations for each step.

Step 1: Refine Your SaaS Idea and Business Plan

Before seeking funding, refine your SaaS idea and develop a comprehensive business plan. This includes:

1. **Idea validation:** Conduct market research, identify your target audience, and assess the potential demand for your SaaS solution.

2. **Value proposition:** Clearly articulate the unique value your SaaS offering brings to customers and differentiate it from competitors.

3. **Business model:** Define your revenue streams, pricing strategy, customer acquisition and retention plans, and go-to-market strategy.

4. **Financial projections:** Create detailed financial projections, including revenue forecasts, expense breakdowns, and key metrics like ARR, CAC, and CLTV.

Step 2: Bootstrap and Self-Funding

Before seeking external capital, consider bootstrapping and self-funding options to demonstrate initial traction and reduce your funding needs. This step involves:

1. **Personal savings:** Use your personal savings to finance early-stage development, minimum viable product (MVP) creation, or initial marketing efforts.

2. **Friends and family:** Approach friends and family for loans, investments, or co-founding partnerships, but ensure clear communication and well-defined terms.

Step 3: Seek Seed Funding from Angel Investors

Angel investors can provide early-stage funding and valuable industry expertise. To attract angel investors, follow these steps:

1. **Build a network:** Attend startup events, pitch competitions, and join entrepreneur networks to connect with potential angel investors.

2. **Develop a compelling pitch:** Craft a persuasive pitch deck that highlights your SaaS idea, market opportunity, competitive advantage, and growth potential.

3. **Research angel investors:** Identify angel investors with a track record of investing in the SaaS industry and aligning with your business goals.

4. **Pitch and negotiate:** Reach out to potential angel investors, schedule meetings or presentations, and be prepared to negotiate terms and valuations.

Step 4: Pursue Venture Capital (VC) Funding

Venture capital firms can provide significant funding for SaaS startups in exchange for equity. Here's how to approach VC funding:

1. **Build a scalable business:** VC investors seek high-growth opportunities, so demonstrate the scalability and market potential of your SaaS business.

2. **Identify suitable VCs:** Research venture capital firms that specialize in SaaS investments and have a successful track record in the industry.

3. **Prepare a strong pitch deck:** Develop a comprehensive pitch deck that includes your market opportunity, competitive landscape, growth strategy, and financial projections.

4. **Seek warm introductions:** Leverage your network, advisors, or angel investors to secure warm introductions to VCs, as these connections can significantly increase your chances of getting a meeting.

Step 5: Consider Strategic Partnerships and Corporate Investments

Strategic partnerships and corporate investments can bring both funding and industry expertise. Follow these steps to explore such opportunities:

1. **Identify potential partners:** Identify companies within your industry or related sectors that could benefit from partnering with or investing in your SaaS startup.

2. **Pitch to strategic partners:** Present your SaaS idea and the value of a partnership, emphasizing the mutual benefits and potential synergies.

3. **Leverage incubators and accelerators:** Apply to industry-specific incubators or accelerators that offer funding, mentorship, and connections to potential corporate partners.

4. **Attend industry events:** Participate in conferences, networking events, and industry forums where you can meet potential partners and investors.

Step 6: Crowdfunding and Online Platforms

Crowdfunding platforms provide an alternative method to raise funds from a large pool of individual investors. Consider these steps for crowdfunding:

1. **Select a crowdfunding platform:** Choose a platform suitable for your SaaS startup, such as Kickstarter, Indiegogo, or equity-based platforms like SeedInvest or AngelList.

2. **Create a compelling campaign:** Craft a persuasive campaign that clearly communicates your SaaS idea, value proposition, and the potential impact it can make.

3. **Engage your network:** Leverage your personal and professional networks to spread the word about your crowdfunding campaign, encouraging supporters to contribute and share.

4. **Offer attractive rewards:** Provide enticing rewards or incentives to backers, such as early access to your SaaS product, exclusive features, or discounts.

Step 7: Secure Government Grants and Startup Competitions

Government grants and startup competitions can provide non-dilutive funding and validation for your SaaS idea. Follow these steps to pursue such opportunities:

1. **Research grants and competitions:** Explore government grants and startup competitions that specifically target technology startups, including SaaS businesses.

2. **Craft strong applications:** Prepare well-written grant proposals or competition entries that clearly articulate your SaaS idea, market opportunity, and growth potential.

3. **Leverage support organizations:** Seek assistance from local business development organizations, entrepreneurship centers, or startup incubators that can guide you in finding relevant grants and competitions.

Raising funds for your SaaS idea requires a well-thought-out strategy and an understanding of the available funding options. By following the steps outlined in this chapter, including refining your idea, seeking seed funding, pursuing venture capital, exploring strategic partnerships, leveraging crowdfunding, and exploring non-dilutive funding sources, you can increase your chances of securing the necessary capital to bring your SaaS startup to life. Remember to tailor your approach to your specific business needs and continually refine your pitch based on feedback and market dynamics.

Notes

NETWORKING FOR FUND RAISING

However, the biggest challenge that any first-time entrepreneur faces is to find connections or network with investors. Here's an additional section on how to find phone numbers or contacts of VC firms or potential investors:

Finding contact information for VC firms or potential investors can require some research and networking efforts. Here are a few strategies to help you find phone numbers or contacts:

1. **Utilize Online Directories and Databases:**

    - **Crunchbase:** Crunchbase is a comprehensive online platform that provides information on companies, investors, and funding rounds. It often includes contact details for venture capital firms and individual investors.

    - **AngelList:** AngelList is a platform connecting startups with investors. It offers a directory of venture capital firms and angel investors, providing contact information and profiles.

    - **LinkedIn:** Utilize LinkedIn's advanced search functionality to identify venture capital firms and individual investors. Connect with them directly or seek mutual connections who can provide introductions.

2. **Attend Networking Events and Conferences:**

    - **Industry events:** Attend conferences, workshops, pitch competitions, and networking events focused on entrepreneurship, startups, or the SaaS industry. These events provide opportunities to meet investors and obtain contact information directly.

    - **Pitch events:** Participate in pitch events or demo days organized by incubators, accelerators, or startup communities. Investors often attend these events, and they may share contact information or express interest in connecting further.

3. **Leverage Warm Introductions and Referrals:**

    - **Seek introductions:** Leverage your existing network, mentors, advisors, or industry contacts to seek warm introductions to potential investors. Personal introductions can significantly increase your chances of connecting with investors and getting a response.

    - **Join startup communities:** Engage with startup communities, angel investor networks, or entrepreneurship organizations that facilitate connections between founders and investors. These communities often offer resources, events, and networking opportunities to connect with potential investors.

4. **Research and Target Specific Investors:**

    - **Research venture capital firms:** Conduct thorough research on venture capital firms that focus on SaaS investments. Visit their websites, explore their portfolio companies, and look for partners or associates responsible for investments in the SaaS sector.

    - **Investor databases:** Use investor databases such as PitchBook, CB Insights, or AngelList Pro to access comprehensive data on venture capital firms and individual investors. These platforms often provide contact information and investment preferences.

5. **Engage with Online Platforms and Social Media:**

    - **Twitter:** Follow venture capital firms and individual investors on Twitter. They often share industry insights, investment updates, and contact information in their profiles or tweets.

    - **AngelList and Gust:** Platforms like AngelList and Gust allow startups to create profiles and directly connect with investors who are actively looking for investment opportunities.

6. **Remember, when contacting investors, it is important to personalize your outreach and demonstrate a clear understanding of their investment focus and portfolio. Craft a concise and compelling message highlighting the value of your SaaS idea and the potential alignment with their investment interests.**

Note: *Respect investor preferences regarding contact methods. Some investors may prefer email communication or have specific channels for submitting investment proposals, so be mindful of their stated preferences.*

By leveraging these strategies, you can increase your chances of finding contact information for venture capital firms and potential investors, helping you connect with them to discuss your SaaS idea and investment opportunities.

Notes

GENERAL VALUATION METHODS

Determining the right valuation for a SaaS business is a complex process that involves multiple factors and considerations. While there is no one-size-fits-all formula, there are various methods commonly used in the valuation of SaaS companies. Here are a few commonly employed valuation approaches:

Let's get into the explanations of revenue-based valuation methods, including Multiple of Annual Recurring Revenue (ARR) and Price-to-Sales (P/S) ratio:

- **Multiple of Annual Recurring Revenue (ARR):** The Multiple of Annual Recurring Revenue (ARR) is a valuation method that calculates the worth of a SaaS company by applying a multiple to its ARR. ARR represents the annual recurring revenue generated by the company's subscription-based business model. Here's how it works:

    - **Determine your company's ARR:** Calculate the total revenue generated from recurring subscriptions over a 12-month period. Exclude one-time or non-recurring revenue sources.

    - **Apply a valuation multiple:** Research industry benchmarks, comparable company valuations, and market conditions to identify an appropriate multiple. The multiple is typically a factor that represents the value investors are willing to pay based on factors like growth rate, market potential, profitability, and risk.

- **Calculate valuation:** Multiply your ARR by the chosen multiple to arrive at the estimated valuation. For example, if your ARR is $1 million and the chosen multiple is 5x, the estimated valuation would be $5 million ($1 million x 5).

The multiple used in the valuation can vary widely depending on several factors, including industry trends, growth rate, profitability, customer retention, competitive landscape, and market conditions. It's crucial to consider these factors to determine a reasonable multiple that aligns with the specific characteristics of your SaaS business.

- **Price-to-Sales (P/S) ratio:** The Price-to-Sales (P/S) ratio is another revenue-based valuation method that compares a company's revenue to its valuation. It is calculated by dividing the company's market capitalization or enterprise value by its total revenue. Here's how it works:

    - **Determine market capitalization or enterprise value:** Market capitalization represents the total market value of a company's outstanding shares, while enterprise value includes market capitalization plus debt and minus cash and cash equivalents.

    - **Calculate the P/S ratio:** Divide the market capitalization or enterprise value by the total revenue. The resulting ratio indicates how much investors are willing to pay for every dollar of revenue generated.

    - **Compare to industry benchmarks:** Research industry benchmarks or comparable companies to assess typical P/S ratios for SaaS businesses. This helps determine if your company's P/S ratio is within a reasonable range.

The P/S ratio is influenced by factors such as growth potential, profitability, market position, competitive landscape, and overall market sentiment. It's important to note that P/S ratios can vary across industries, with high-growth sectors like SaaS often commanding higher ratios.

Both the Multiple of ARR and P/S ratio provide a simplified method for valuing a SaaS company based on its revenue. However, it's crucial to consider other factors such as growth prospects, profitability, market share, competitive advantages, and market conditions to arrive at a more comprehensive and accurate valuation. Consulting with a financial advisor or valuation expert can help you navigate the nuances of these methods and arrive at a well-informed valuation.

1. Market-based valuation:

- **Comparable Company Analysis:** Research and compare the valuations of similar SaaS companies in the market. Analyze their financial metrics, growth rates, market share, and other relevant factors to estimate your own valuation. Here's how it works:
    - **Identify comparable companies:** Look for publicly traded SaaS companies or private SaaS companies with available valuation information that are similar in terms of business model, target market, growth stage, and other relevant factors.
    - **Analyze financial metrics:** Gather financial information, such as revenue, profitability, growth rates, and key performance indicators, for the identified comparable companies.
    - **Assess market factors:** Consider the competitive landscape, market share, customer base, and industry trends that impact the valuations of the comparable companies.
    - **Apply valuation multiples:** Calculate valuation multiples based on financial metrics, such as Price-to-Earnings (P/E) ratio, Price-to-Sales (P/S) ratio, or Enterprise Value-to-Revenue (EV/Revenue) ratio, for the comparable companies.
    - **Estimate your valuation:** Apply the valuation multiples from the comparable companies to your own financial metrics. Multiply your revenue, earnings, or other relevant factors by the corresponding multiples to estimate your own valuation.

For example, if you identify a comparable SaaS company with a P/S ratio of 8 and your SaaS company has $2 million in annual revenue, your estimated valuation would be $16 million ($2 million x 8).

The Comparable Company Analysis relies on the assumption that similar companies in the same industry should have similar valuations. However, it's important to consider the differences in growth rates, market position, profitability, and other factors when selecting and comparing comparable companies.

- **Precedent Transaction Analysis:** Examine the valuations of recent acquisitions or funding rounds in the SaaS industry. Consider similar companies' valuations and apply them to your own business. Comparable Company Analysis is a valuation method that involves researching and comparing the valuations of similar SaaS companies in the market to estimate your own valuation. Here's how it works:
    - **Identify comparable companies:** Look for publicly traded SaaS companies or private SaaS companies with available valuation information that are similar in terms of business model, target market, growth stage, and other relevant factors.
    - **Analyze financial metrics**: Gather financial information, such as revenue, profitability, growth rates, and key performance indicators, for the identified comparable companies.
    - **Assess market factors:** Consider the competitive landscape, market share, customer base, and industry trends that impact the valuations of the comparable companies.
    - **Apply valuation multiples:** Calculate valuation multiples based on financial metrics, such as Price-to-Earnings (P/E) ratio, Price-to-Sales (P/S) ratio, or Enterprise Value-to-Revenue (EV/Revenue) ratio, for the comparable companies.
    - **Estimate your valuation:** Apply the valuation multiples from the comparable companies to your own financial metrics. Multiply your revenue, earnings, or other relevant factors by the corresponding multiples to estimate your own valuation.

For example, if you identify a comparable SaaS company with a P/S ratio of 8 and your SaaS company has $2 million in annual revenue, your estimated valuation would be $16 million ($2 million x 8).

The Comparable Company Analysis relies on the assumption that similar companies in the same industry should have similar valuations. However, it's important to consider the differences in growth rates, market position, profitability, and other factors when selecting and comparing comparable companies.

Discounted Cash Flow (DCF) analysis:

Discounted Cash Flow (DCF) analysis is a valuation method that estimates the value of a SaaS company by assessing its future cash flows and discounting them to their present value. Here's how the DCF analysis works:

- Estimate the future cash flows your SaaS company is expected to generate over a specific period.

  - **Project future cash flows:** Forecast the cash flows your SaaS company is expected to generate over a specific period, typically five to ten years. This projection should include both revenue and expenses, including operating costs, marketing expenses, and capital expenditures.

  - **Consider growth rates:** Estimate the growth rates for your revenue and expenses based on market trends, industry benchmarks, and your company's growth trajectory. Consider factors such as market size, competition, customer acquisition, and retention rates.

  - **Terminal value:** Determine a terminal value, which represents the value of your SaaS company beyond the projection period. This value is usually calculated based on a terminal growth rate applied to the estimated cash flows beyond the projection period.

- Determine an appropriate discount rate that reflects the risks and opportunity costs associated with the investment.

  - **Select a discount rate:** Determine a discount rate that reflects the risks and opportunity costs associated with the investment in your SaaS company. The discount rate represents the required rate of return investors expect for investing in your business.

    - **Consider risk factors:** Factors influencing the discount rate include the SaaS industry's risk profile, company-specific risks, macroeconomic conditions, and the opportunity cost of investing in alternative investments.

- Discount the projected cash flows to their present value to arrive at the valuation.

    - **Apply the discount rate:** Apply the discount rate to each projected cash flow, reducing its value to its present value. The discounting process accounts for the time value of money, reflecting that cash received in the future is worth less than cash received today.
    - **Sum the present values:** Sum up the present values of all projected cash flows, including the terminal value, to arrive at the total present value of the estimated cash flows.
    - **Subtract debt and add cash:** Adjust the present value by subtracting any outstanding debt and adding the value of cash or cash equivalents held by your company.
    - **Calculate the valuation:** The resulting present value represents the estimated valuation of your SaaS company.

DCF analysis is based on the principle that the value of a business is determined by the cash flows it generates over time. By discounting future cash flows to their present value, the analysis provides a fair estimate of the intrinsic value of your SaaS company.

It's important to note that DCF analysis involves making assumptions and forecasts about future performance, which can introduce uncertainties. Sensitivity analysis and considering different scenarios can help evaluate the impact of varying assumptions on the valuation.

Due to the complexity of DCF analysis, seeking the assistance of a financial advisor or valuation expert experienced in conducting DCF valuations can provide more accurate results and insights. They can help you navigate the nuances of cash flow forecasting, discount rate selection, and terminal value determination to arrive at a well-informed valuation for your SaaS company.

Stage-based valuation: Early-stage startups may use methods like the Risk Factor Summation Method or the Scorecard Method to assign values based on specific risk factors, team experience, market potential, intellectual property, and other relevant aspects.

Let's delve into the explanation of stage-based valuation and discuss the different stages of a SaaS company along with their impact on valuation:

Stage-based valuation is a method used by early-stage startups to assign values based on specific risk factors, team experience, market potential, intellectual property, and other relevant aspects. Two commonly used methods within stage-based valuation are the Risk Factor Summation Method and the Scorecard Method. Here's an overview of these methods:

2. Risk Factor Summation Method:

The Risk Factor Summation Method assigns a value to a startup based on a comprehensive assessment of various risk factors associated with the business. Each risk factor is assigned a score or weight, and the cumulative score is used to estimate the valuation. Here's how it works:

- **Identify key risk factors:** Identify and assess specific risk factors that are relevant to your SaaS business, such as market adoption, competition, product development, team experience, intellectual property, funding, or regulatory risks.

- **Assign weights or scores:** Assign weights or scores to each risk factor based on its perceived impact on the business's valuation. Higher weights indicate higher risks.

- **Calculate the risk factor score:** Sum up the scores or weighted values for all risk factors to arrive at the risk factor score.

- **Determine the valuation:** Apply a predetermined formula or valuation multiplier to the risk factor score to estimate the valuation. The multiplier reflects the average valuation impact of each risk point.

The Risk Factor Summation Method provides a systematic approach to evaluating the risks and opportunities associated with a startup. It helps investors and founders better understand the valuation drivers and allocate value based on risk exposure.

3. Scorecard Method:

The Scorecard Method assesses the startup's value by comparing it to other startups in similar stages and industries. It assigns weights to various factors, such as team, market potential, product, and intellectual property, and calculates a weighted average score to estimate the valuation. Here's how it works:

Identify relevant factors: Identify key factors that contribute to the valuation, such as team experience, market potential, product differentiation, intellectual property, or traction.

- **Assign weights:** Assign weights to each factor based on their importance and relevance to the business. These weights are usually determined based on industry norms or expert judgment.

- **Assess each factor:** Evaluate the startup's performance or characteristics related to each factor and assign scores accordingly.

- **Calculate the weighted average score:** Multiply each factor's score by its assigned weight and calculate the weighted average score.

- **Determine the valuation:** Apply a predetermined formula or valuation multiplier to the weighted average score to estimate the valuation.

The Scorecard Method helps provide a structured approach to comparing the startup's value to similar companies and considering the relative strengths and weaknesses across different evaluation factors.

Now, let's discuss the different stages of a SaaS company and their impact on valuation:

- **Seed Stage:** At the seed stage, the company is in its early development phase, focusing on validating the business idea and building a minimum viable product (MVP). Valuations at this stage are typically lower due to the higher risks involved and the limited progress made. Investors primarily evaluate the team's capabilities, market potential, and intellectual property.

- **Early Stage:** In the early stage, the company has developed its product or service and is starting to acquire initial customers. Valuations in this stage are influenced by factors such as market adoption, revenue growth, customer feedback, and product-market fit. Investors assess the scalability and growth potential of the business.

- **Growth Stage**: At the growth stage, the company has achieved significant customer traction and is scaling its operations. Valuations at this stage can increase substantially, driven by factors like revenue growth rate, market share, customer retention, profitability, and expansion plans. Investors focus on assessing the company's ability to achieve sustained growth and market leadership.

- **Maturity Stage:** In the late stage, the company has established itself as a market leader and aims to further expand its market share or explore exit opportunities. Valuations are influenced by factors such as revenue size, profitability, competitive position, intellectual property portfolio, and strategic partnerships. Investors assess the company's potential for a successful exit or IPO.

It's important to note that valuation at each stage is subject to market conditions, investor sentiment, and the specific characteristics of the company. The valuation can increase or decrease as the company progresses through different stages based on its performance, market dynamics, and investor perception.

Understanding the different stages of a SaaS company and their impact on valuation helps entrepreneurs and investors gauge the appropriate valuation range based on the company's progress, growth prospects, and risk profile.

It's important to note that valuation is subjective and can vary based on factors such as market conditions, investor sentiment, growth potential, competitive landscape, and more. Seeking the assistance of a financial advisor or valuation expert with expertise in the SaaS industry can provide a more accurate and comprehensive valuation based on specific market dynamics and industry standards.

Remember that valuations are estimates, and the ultimate valuation will depend on negotiations between the company and potential investors or acquirers.

ASSESSING THE GROWTH STAGE OF YOUR SAAS STARTUP

Key Indicators and Considerations

Determining the stage of your SaaS startup requires assessing various factors related to your business's growth, customer base, and market presence. Here are some key indicators to help you identify the stage of your SaaS startup:

1. **Product Development**: Evaluate the stage of your product development process. If you are in the early stages of building a minimum viable product (MVP) and validating the market need, you are likely in the seed stage. If you have a developed product or service and are acquiring initial customers, you are likely in the early stage.

2. **Customer Acquisition:** Assess the number and growth rate of your customer base. In the seed stage, you may have a limited number of early adopters or pilot customers. As you start acquiring more customers and experiencing significant growth in user adoption, you may transition into the growth stage.

3. **Revenue Generation:** Consider your revenue generation capabilities. In the seed and early stages, revenue may be limited or primarily driven by early customer contracts or pilot programs. In the growth stage, you should be experiencing consistent revenue growth and potentially reaching profitability.

4. **Market Share and Competition:** Evaluate your market position and competition. In the seed stage, you may still be exploring your target market and establishing your unique value proposition. In the growth stage, you should have gained a significant market share and be competing with established players or experiencing competition from emerging competitors.

5. **Funding and Investment:** Consider your funding status and investor interest. In the seed stage, you may be actively seeking seed funding or early-stage investments. As you progress through the stages, you may have secured funding rounds from angel investors or venture capitalists, indicating investor confidence in your growth potential.

6. **Operational Scale:** Assess the scale of your operations and infrastructure. In the seed stage, your operations may be lean, with a focus on testing and refining your product. As you enter the growth stage, you should be scaling your operations, expanding your team, and investing in infrastructure to support increasing customer demand.

7. **Market Maturity:** Evaluate the maturity of your target market. If you are operating in a niche or emerging market with significant growth potential, you may be in the early or growth stage. If you are in a mature market with established competitors and slower growth rates, you may be in the maturity stage.

It's important to note that these indicators are general guidelines, and the transition between stages can be gradual and subjective. Your specific circumstances and industry dynamics may influence the timing and progression through each stage. Regularly reassessing your business's growth and considering these indicators will help you better understand the stage of your SaaS startup and inform strategic decision-making.

However, to showcase the stage of your SaaS startup to investors, consider the following approach:

- **Clearly define the stage:** Describe the stage of your startup by assessing your product development progress, customer acquisition, revenue generation, market share, funding status, operational scale, and market maturity. Provide a concise overview of each aspect.

- **Highlight milestones and achievements:** Showcase key milestones and achievements that demonstrate your progress in each stage. This can include successful product launches, customer acquisition milestones, revenue growth, market share expansion, funding rounds, operational advancements, and market validation.

- **Present data and metrics:** Back up your claims with data and metrics relevant to each stage. Provide metrics such as customer growth rate, revenue figures, market share data, funding raised, operational metrics, and market analysis to support your assertions and provide concrete evidence of your performance.

- **Emphasize growth potential:** Clearly communicate the growth potential of your startup based on your current stage and market dynamics. Highlight market opportunities, competitive advantages, and strategies to capture a larger market share, expand revenue streams, and drive future growth.

- **Showcase team expertise:** Highlight the expertise and experience of your team members to instill confidence in investors. Showcase key team members' backgrounds, relevant industry experience, and track record in successfully navigating startups through different stages.

- **Provide a roadmap:** Outline your future plans and growth strategy for the next stage. Demonstrate a clear understanding of the challenges and opportunities ahead, and explain how you plan to capitalize on them. Present a well-thought-out roadmap that aligns with investor expectations and showcases your ability to execute.

- **Communicate your ask:** Clearly state your funding needs and investment requirements. Specify how the funds will be utilized to fuel growth, capture market opportunities, and achieve key milestones. Be transparent about the investment terms and expected returns to align investor expectations with your business objectives.

By presenting a comprehensive overview of your startup's stage, milestones, metrics, growth potential, team expertise, future plans, and funding requirements, you can effectively showcase your SaaS startup to investors and demonstrate why they should invest in your business.

CAUTIONS

The following page serves as a general cautionary statement to readers of this book. It is important to acknowledge that the information contained within this book is provided for educational and informational purposes only. The content presented is based on general knowledge and understanding up to September 2021, and it may not reflect the most current updates or developments in the field of SaaS marketing. Readers are advised to conduct their own research and consult with professionals or experts for specific advice or guidance related to their individual circumstances.

No Legal or Professional Advice

The information presented in this book is not intended to serve as legal, financial, or professional advice. While efforts have been made to ensure the accuracy and reliability of the information provided, the author and publisher make no claims, promises, or guarantees about the completeness, accuracy, or suitability of the content. Readers should not rely solely on the information presented in this book and should seek professional advice from qualified experts or consultants regarding their specific situations.

Use of Trademarks and Copyrighted Material

Throughout this book, certain trademarks, product names, company names, and copyrighted material may be mentioned. The inclusion of such material is for illustrative purposes only and does not imply endorsement, affiliation, or sponsorship by the respective owners. The author and publisher do not intend to infringe upon any intellectual property rights, and any use of trademarks or copyrighted material is done in accordance with fair use guidelines. Readers are advised to respect intellectual property rights and seek appropriate permissions or licenses when using third-party material.

Speculative Commentary and Future Predictions

In certain chapters or sections, the author may provide speculative commentary, predictions, or insights regarding SaaS marketing, industry trends, or emerging technologies. These speculations are based on the author's personal interpretation and assessment and should not be considered as factual or guaranteed. The future is inherently uncertain, and actual outcomes may differ from the author's predictions. Readers are encouraged to exercise their own judgment and conduct additional research before making any business decisions based on speculative commentary or predictions.

Limitation of Liability

The author and publisher of this book disclaim any liability for any loss, damage, or injury caused by the use or reliance upon the information presented herein. The content provided is on an "as-is" basis without warranties of any kind, express or implied. The author and publisher shall not be held responsible for any direct, indirect, incidental, consequential, or special damages arising out of or in connection with the use of this book.

Personal Responsibility

Readers are solely responsible for the interpretation and application of the information presented in this book. The author and publisher cannot be held liable for any decisions, actions, or outcomes resulting from the implementation of the ideas or strategies discussed. It is essential for readers to exercise their own discretion, perform due diligence, and seek professional advice when necessary to ensure the suitability and effectiveness of any strategies or recommendations provided.

In conclusion, this caution page serves as a reminder that the content presented in this book is intended for general information purposes only. Readers are encouraged to exercise their own judgment, conduct independent research, and seek professional advice before making any business or investment decisions. The author and publisher disclaim any responsibility for the accuracy, completeness, or applicability of the information contained within this book.